500 RECIPES FOR COOKING FOR TWO

by Katie Stewart

Contents

Published by Hamlyn Publishing
a division of The Hamlyn Publishing Group Limited
Astronaut House, Feltham, Middlesex, England

© Copyright Katie Stewart 1965
ISBN 0 600 31707 2

First printed 1965
Revised edition 1971
Sixteenth impression 1984

Printed and bound in Great Britain by
R. J. Acford

Introduction

Millions of people are faced almost every day with the problem of cooking for two. It will not be news to them that preparing meals for such a small number is indeed a problem in itself. Until recently I was one of the many who had to try to put variety and interest into meals for two on a budget which at best could be described as economic. Experience taught me that with careful thought and planning the task could be made both interesting and rewarding. So I welcomed the opportunity to write this book and pass on my discoveries of the many fascinating recipes which can be made suitable for two.

I have divided the book into sections, each dealing with a particular situation, but I hope that when you are searching for ideas you will look through all the sections, since there are many ideas which are interchangeable.

I have also included some advice on shopping for two, and a glossary of some of the terms used in this book.

Cover photograph by

D1324650

HAMLYN

Useful information on cooking for two

Shopping for two

There are few of us who can afford to ignore the cost of living and it's so much easier to waste money by over-spending when cooking for two than for a greater number. For this reason careful shopping is of the greatest importance. To save yourself time and trouble, buy a stock of dry groceries at weekends so you need only shop for perishable foods during the week. Try to work out which meals you have to cater for, and what food you are going to prepare, at the beginning of the week.

I find that a list that I have drawn up for myself of meals that are easy, economical and quick, and which I have fixed on the back of my larder door, serves as an excellent reminder for ideas.

Cookery terms

Mixed seasoning – a mixture to flavour soups, stews, casseroles and sauces, very handy if kept ready-made in the kitchen. Mix together 8 oz. salt, 1 level tablespoon pepper and 1 level teaspoon ground mace. Store in an air-tight jar.

Seasoned flour – recommended when flour is used for coating meat, poultry or fish before cooking. Measure on to a flat surface using 1 rounded tablespoon flour to 1 level teaspoon salt and ½ level teaspoon pepper. Mix well and use.

Bouquet garni – small bundle of herbs to flavour soups, stews and casseroles. It consists of 1 small bay leaf, a sprig of thyme and a few parsley stalks, tied together with cotton. Remove before serving the dish – it is a good idea to tie the other end of the thread to the pan handle, then it can easily be found to lift out.

Fresh white breadcrumbs – remove the crusts from bread slices at least a day old and rub the bread through a fine wire sieve or simply rub between the fingers. These breadcrumbs will not keep unless thoroughly dried off in a very cool oven, then stored in a screw-top jar.

Some Useful Facts and Figures

Notes on metrication

In case you wish to convert quantities into metric measures, the following tables give a comparison.

Solid measures

Ounces	Approx. grams to nearest whole figure	Recommended conversion to nearest unit of 25
1	28	25
2	57	50
3	85	75
4	113	100
5	142	150
6	170	175
7	198	200
8	227	225
9	255	250
10	283	275
11	312	300
12	340	350
13	368	375
14	396	400
15	425	425
16 (1 lb)	454	450
17	482	475
18	510	500
19	539	550
20 (1¼ lb)	567	575

Note: When converting quantities over 20 oz first add the appropriate figures in the centre column, then adjust to the nearest unit of 25. As a general guide, 1 kg (1000 g) equals 2·2 lb or about 2 lb 3 oz. This method of conversion gives good results in nearly all cases, although in certain pastry and cake recipes a more accurate conversion is necessary to produce a balanced recipe.

Liquid measures

Imperial	Approx. millilitres to nearest whole figure	Recommended millilitres
¼ pint	142	150
½ pint	283	300
¾ pint	425	450
1 pint	567	600
1½ pints	851	900
1¾ pints	992	1000 (1 litre)

Oven temperatures

The table below gives recommended equivalents.

	°C	°F	Gas Mark
Very cool	110	225	¼
	120	250	½
Cool	140	275	1
	150	300	2
Moderate	160	325	3
	180	350	4
Moderately hot	190	375	5
	200	400	6
Hot	220	425	7
	230	450	8
Very hot	240	475	9

Notes for American and Australian users

In America the 8-oz measuring cup is used. In Australia metric measures are now used in conjunction with the standard 250-ml measuring cup. The Imperial pint, used in Britain and Australia, is 20 fl oz, while the American pint is 16 fl oz. It is important to remember that the Australian tablespoon differs from both the British and American tablespoons. The British standard tablespoon, which has been used throughout this book, holds 17·7 ml, the American 14·2 ml, and the Australian 20 ml. A teaspoon holds approximately 5 ml in all three countries.

Basic pastry recipes

Simple short crust or flaky pastry is used in many of the recipes in this book. Do remember when a recipe calls for a quantity of pastry – for instance 4 oz. of short crust pastry, the quantity refers to the weight of the flour only, not all the ingredients added together. Therefore 4 oz. short crust pastry means a pastry made up using 4 oz. flour and 2 oz. fat, etc.

Plain short crust pastry

makes 4 oz. pastry

you will need:

4 oz. plain flour	2 tablespoons milk OR
pinch salt	water to mix
2 oz. mixed fats (equal quantities butter, margarine and vegetable fat)	

1 Sift together the flour and salt into a basin. Measure the fat on to a plate. Using a knife blade, beat down the fats and mix until soft and blended. Add all at once to the flour.
2 Using the tips of the fingers (the coolest part of the hands) gently break the fat into small lumps, then rub into the flour in order to blend the two together very finely and thoroughly. To 'rub in' means to pick up small handfuls of the mixture and rub very lightly with the thumbs so that the mixture falls back through the fingers into the basin. The action not only blends together the fat and the flour but also incorporates air which eventually results in a light pastry. It is equally important not to overmix the pastry at any stage, and rubbing in should stop when the mixture looks crumbly.
3 Add the liquid, all at once, into the centre of the mixture. Blend using a fork, until the mixture clings together into a ball, leaving the sides of the basin clean. Turn out on to a lightly floured surface and knead lightly to make a smooth fairly stiff dough.
4 Set the pastry aside to rest for 10 minutes before using. For baking time see recipes.

Sweet short crust pastry

makes 4 oz. pastry

you will need:

4 oz. plain flour	1 level tablespoon
pinch salt	castor sugar mixed
2 oz. mixed fats	with 1½ level table-spoons milk

Prepare the pastry, following instructions, above,

for plain short crust. Use for sweet pies, tarts, flans and turnovers. For baking time see recipes.

Cheese pastry

makes 4 oz. pastry

you will need:

4 oz. plain flour	1 oz. cheese, finely
pinch salt and cayenne pepper	grated
2 oz. mixed fats OR butter	2–3 tablespoons milk OR egg and milk

Prepare the pastry as for plain short crust instructions. Use for savoury flans, tartlet cases and for cheese straws and biscuits. For baking time see recipes.

Flaky pastry

makes 8 oz. pastry

you will need:

8 oz. plain flour	¼ pint (about 6 table-spoons) water
½ level teaspoon salt	1 teaspoon vinegar OR lemon juice
6 oz. butter OR margarine and lard (equal quantities)	

1 Sift together the flour and salt into a basin and set aside.
2 With a knife mix the fats together on a plate until softened and blended. Spread evenly over the plate into four equal portions.
3 Rub one portion into the sieved flour.
4 Mix water and vinegar and add to mixture to form a smooth dough. Leave to rest for 10 minutes before rolling out.
5 Roll out the dough to an oblong shape, about 3 times as long as it is wide. Place one-third of the remaining fat in small pieces over two-thirds of the dough, distributing the fat evenly with spaces between pieces. Mark the pastry into thirds and fold the lower uncovered section over the centre and the top down over both.
6 Give a half-turn so that one of the open edges faces you. Seal edges and roll out again.
7 Repeat and rest the dough 10 minutes between each turn until all the fat has been added.
8 Roll and fold once more and then leave in a cool place 20 minutes before using.

How to make a hearty breakfast

I'm a great breakfast fan. I believe that a hearty breakfast is a sound basis for a day's hard work, whether at the office or at home. If you've little time for preparation, set the table and prepare as much of the food as possible the night before. Allow as much time as possible for eating, and vary the menu as much as possible – begin with porridge, cereal, stewed fruit or fruit juice and then follow up with a main dish, toast and marmalade and a hot drink.

How to make coffee

Measure 1½–2 oz. (2 heaped tablespoons) medium-ground coffee into a heated jug. Add a pinch of salt and allow the grounds to warm gently to draw out the flavour.
Measure 1 pint cold water into a kettle and bring to the boil. Pour over the coffee immediately and stir well. Cover with a cloth or a saucer and leave to stand for 4–5 minutes. Strain it through muslin into a heated coffee pot or clean jug.
In a saucepan – measure 1½–2 oz. (or heaped tablespoons) medium-ground coffee into saucepan. Add a pinch of salt and 1 pint cold water. Stir well and bring just to the boil. Remove from the heat immediately, stir again, cover with a lid and set aside in a warm place to infuse for 4–5 minutes. Strain into a heated coffee pot or jug and serve.
In a percolator – measure 1 pint cold water into the lower half of the percolator and 1½–2 oz. medium-ground coffee into the top perforated section. Heat gently and allow to bubble through the coffee for about 6 minutes. Remove from the heat and serve.
Instant coffee – allow about 1 teaspoon for each person. Either make in the cup or measure the required quantity into a heated jug and pour sufficient, almost boiling water over. Stir, then serve.
In all cases heat the required milk separately and serve with the hot coffee in a separate jug.

Porridge

you will need:

1 pint water	¼ level teaspoon salt
2 rounded tablespoons medium oatmeal	

1 The night before, measure the water, oatmeal and salt into a saucepan. Leave to soak overnight.

2 Bring to the boil, stirring all the time. Lower the heat and leave to simmer for 15 minutes, stirring occasionally.
3 Serve hot with creamy milk and sugar or a sprinkling of salt.

Prunes

you will need:

4 oz. prunes	1 tablespoon brown sugar
brewed tea	
little lemon peel	

1 Place the prunes in a basin and cover with tea. There is no need to make an extra pot – simply refill the pot containing used leaves with hot water, allow to stand for a few minutes, then strain over the prunes.
2 Leave to soak overnight.
3 Next day place prunes and liquid in a saucepan, add a small piece of lemon peel and simmer gently until tender.
4 Remove the peel and stir in the sugar before serving, warm or cold.

Stewed fresh fruit

you will need:

8 oz. apples OR rhubarb	¼ pint water
	little grated lemon rind
1–2 oz. castor sugar	OR ginger

1 Peel and slice the apples, or scrub and cut the rhubarb into 1-inch lengths.
2 Measure the sugar and water into a saucepan and stir over a low heat to dissolve the sugar.
3 Add the prepared fruit, cover with a lid and place over very low heat. Allow to cook slowly until the fruit is tender but still whole.
4 Draw the pan off the heat and add a little finely grated lemon rind to apples (or a pinch of ginger to rhubarb) and set aside to cool.
5 Spoon into a serving dish and chill until ready to serve.

Muesli

you will need:

1 heaped tablespoon quick-cooking oats	1 oz. seedless raisins
scant ¼ pint water	1 tablespoon chopped walnuts
juice 1 lemon	2 eating apples (sharp flavoured)
1 heaped tablespoon sweetened condensed milk	

1 Measure the oats into a small basin, add the water and leave to soak overnight. *continued*

2 Next morning stir in the lemon juice, condensed milk and dried fruit.

3 Just before serving, stir in the chopped walnuts and the apples (grated with skin on) and spoon into two serving dishes.

Chicken livers on toast

you will need:

¼ lb. fresh (or 3-oz. packet frozen) chicken livers	1 oz. butter OR margarine
	2 slices bread
seasoned flour	squeeze of lemon juice

1 If frozen, thaw and separate the chicken livers. Trim away any core and roll in seasoned flour.

2 Fry in hot butter for 2–3 minutes until browned.

3 Meanwhile toast bread and butter.

4 Add a squeeze of lemon juice to livers, then lift out on to the slices of hot buttered toast and serve.

Finnan haddock with poached eggs

you will need:

2 small finnan haddock	2 eggs
milk to cover	salt and pepper
½ oz. butter	

1 Cut off the tail and place the fish in a shallow pan.

2 Cover with milk and add butter. Bring to the boil, draw pan off the heat, cover and leave 5 minutes.

3 Meanwhile poach the eggs in simmering salted water.

4 Drain the fish, put on a serving dish, season with salt and pepper and top with drained poached eggs. Serve at once.

Grilled kippers

you will need:

2 kippers	butter for serving

1 Holding the kipper closed, cut off the head and tail from each.

2 Open out on to the base of the grill pan or flat baking tray, skin side downwards.

3 Place under a moderate heat and cook for 5–6 minutes, until the kipper is well heated through.

4 Serve at once with a pat of butter (if liked, the bone can be removed before serving).

Jugged kippers

you will need:

2 kippers	butter for serving

1 Cut the heads and tails from the kippers and place in a jug or deep dish.

2 Pour over boiling water to cover, and leave to stand for 10 minutes.

3 Drain and serve with a large lump of butter in the centre of each.

French toast and bacon

you will need:

1 egg	2 slices day-old bread
pinch salt	1 oz. butter for frying
2 tablespoons milk	2–4 bacon rashers
1 level teaspoon castor sugar	

1 Crack egg into a dish, add salt, milk and sugar and whisk thoroughly with a fork.

2 Dip both sides of each bread slice in the mixture and fry at once in the hot butter, frying both sides until golden brown.

3 Meanwhile trim and grill bacon rashers. Serve with the French toast.

Bacon fritters with tomatoes

makes about 6 fritters

you will need:

4 rashers bacon	salt and pepper
½ oz. dripping OR vegetable shortening	1 egg, lightly mixed
	milk to mix
2 oz. self-raising flour	2 tomatoes

1 Trim and chop the bacon rashers. Fry in the hot fat until crisp, remove and drain.

2 Sieve the flour into a small basin, season well and stir in the egg and enough milk to mix to a smooth creamy consistency.

3 Stir in the fried bacon and place spoonfuls of the mixture into the hot fat. Fry quickly until golden brown on one side, then flip over and fry on the other side.

4 Meanwhile add the seasoned halved tomatoes, to one side of the pan, and fry. Serve with the bacon fritters.

Baked eggs in cream

you will need:

½ oz. butter	2 tablespoons single cream
2 standard eggs	
salt and pepper	

1 Preheat the oven (400°F. – Gas Mark 6). Place a nut of butter in the base of two ramekin dishes and melt in the oven.

2 Break an egg into each dish, season with salt and pepper and carefully place 1 tablespoon cream over each.

3 Replace in the centre of the oven and bake for 8–10 minutes or until set. Serve at once.

Variations

Baked eggs with herbs – follow the recipe given before, adding a little chopped fresh parsley or chives with the cream.

Baked eggs with mushrooms – sauté 4 sliced button mushrooms in ½ oz. butter with a squeeze of lemon juice. Place these in the dishes first, then continue with the recipe as given.

Savoury egg toast

you will need:

1 egg	yeast extract
3 tablespoons milk	4 slices of bread
salt and pepper	butter for frying

1 Break the egg into a basin, add the milk and seasoning and whisk thoroughly, then strain into a large shallow dish.
2 Spread a little yeast extract on both sides of the bread and soak the bread both sides in the egg mixture.
3 Heat the butter in a large frying pan and, when bubbling, add soaked bread slices very carefully and fry quickly on both sides until golden brown.
4 Cut diagonally and serve at once.

Stuffed mushrooms

you will need:

4 large open mush-
rooms

for the stuffing:

2 bacon rashers	1 teaspoon chopped
2 heaped tablespoons	parsley
fresh white bread-	salt and pepper
crumbs	1 oz. butter, melted

1 Rinse the mushrooms, remove the stalks and place cap side down in a well-buttered baking dish.
2 Chop the mushroom stalks finely. Trim and finely chop the bacon rashers, and add to the mushroom stalks with the breadcrumbs, parsley, seasoning and melted butter. Mix with a fork until moist and crumbly.
3 Pile the mixture into the centre of each mushroom.
4 Place in the centre of a hot oven (400°F. – Gas Mark 6) and bake for 20 minutes. Serve with juices from the dish poured over.

Mushrooms on toast

you will need:

4 oz. mushrooms	1 oz. butter
salt and pepper	2 slices bread

1 Wash and trim the mushrooms, remove the stalks and place cap side down in a well-buttered baking dish.

2 Season and dot with butter.
3 Cover, place in the centre of a hot oven (400°F. – Gas Mark 6), and bake for 15 minutes.
4 Toast the bread.
5 Lift the mushrooms on to the toast slices, pour over the juice from the baking dish and serve.

Sweetbreads and mushrooms on skewers

you will need:

8 oz. calf's sweet-	3 thin rashers streaky
breads	bacon
½ pint cold water	8 small mushrooms
1 level teaspoon salt	1 oz. butter, melted
1 dessertspoon lemon	
juice OR vinegar	

1 Clean the sweetbreads under running cold water. Measure the water, salt and lemon juice into a saucepan and bring to the boil.
2 Add the sweetbreads and simmer for 45 minutes or until tender. Drain and plunge into cold water to harden for 15 minutes.
3 Drain and remove the skin and membrane, cut into chunky pieces and wrap each with a piece of trimmed bacon rasher.
4 Place on skewers, alternately with mushrooms, brush with melted butter and place under a moderate grill for 5–6 minutes, turning to cook evenly. Serve at once.

Corn fritters with bacon

makes 6 fritters

you will need:

1 7-oz. tin whole-	1 rounded tablespoon
kernel sweet corn	flour
salt and pepper	1–2 oz. butter for frying
1 egg	4 bacon rashers

1 Drain the sweet corn and empty into a basin. Season well then stir in the egg, flour and mix to a creamy batter.
2 Heat some of the butter in a pan and add spoonfuls of the sweet corn batter. Fry over moderate heat until brown on one side, then flip over and brown the second side. Add more butter if necessary, to cook remaining mixture.
3 Keep the fritters warm and fry the trimmed bacon rashers quickly, then serve both together.

Bananas wrapped in bacon

you will need:

2 bananas	4 bacon rashers
½ lemon	1 oz. butter for frying
castor sugar	

1 Peel bananas and slice in half. Sprinkle with

lemon juice, roll in castor sugar to coat lightly.
2 Wrap each banana half in trimmed bacon rashers and secure with a wooden cocktail stick.
3 Fry in hot butter over moderate heat until the bacon is crisp and banana heated through and soft. Serve at once.

Gammon steak mixed grill

you will need:

1 gammon steak ½-inch thick	2 oz. mushrooms, trimmed
milk to soak	melted butter OR oil
4 chipolata sausages	
1 tomato	**to garnish:**
	watercress

1 Trim the gammon steak and snip fat at ½-inch intervals, to prevent buckling while cooking. Soak in cold milk or water for 1 hour, then drain and pat dry.
2 Arrange the gammon and sausages on the grill pan, brush the lean part of the gammon and the sausages with a little melted butter or oil and grill at least 3 inches below a moderate heat.
3 Grill for 15–20 minutes, turning the gammon once and the sausages more often. After 10 minutes, add the tomato cut in halves, and mushrooms, to the grill pan, season and brush with melted butter or oil.
4 When cooked slice the gammon in half and serve with rest of grill, garnished with watercress.

Scrambled eggs on toast

you will need:

3 eggs	**to garnish:**
3 tablespoons milk	chopped chives OR
salt and pepper	parsley
¼ oz. butter	
2 slices bread	

1 Measure the eggs, milk and seasoning into a basin. Beat together with a fork.
2 Heat the butter in a small saucepan and strain in the beaten egg mixture.
3 Stir over low heat and keep moving the egg from the bottom of the pan as it sets.
4 Toast the bread and butter.
5 When the mixture is set but still creamy, spoon out at once on to slices of hot buttered toast – if left in the pan it will continue cooking and become dry. Garnish.

Fried scallops

you will need:

3 large scallops	flour to coat
salt and pepper	2 oz. butter
milk	½ lemon

1 Cut the prepared scallops into thick slices and season.

2 Dip first into a little milk and then flour. Fry in hot butter for 6–8 minutes, turning to brown evenly.
3 Draw the pan off the heat, and add squeeze of lemon juice.
4 Serve the scallops with the butter from the pan poured over.

Herring roes on toast

you will need:

4 oz. fresh (or 1 4-oz. packet frozen) herring roes	salt and pepper
	½ oz. butter OR margarine
1 tablespoon porridge oats	2 slices bread
	2 lemon wedges

1 Wash the herring roes in salted water, drain and toss in the seasoned oats.
2 Melt the butter or margarine in a frying pan and add the roes. Fry over low heat for about 5 minutes, turning for even cooking.
3 Meanwhile make toast and butter.
4 Lift roes from the pan and serve on toast. Garnish with a wedge of lemon.

Grilled bacon and kidneys

you will need:

2 bacon rashers	melted butter for grilling
2 lamb's kidneys	

1 Trim rashers. Remove any fat from the kidneys, slice in two and snip out the core.
2 Brush the kidneys with a little melted butter (skewering, if wished, to keep flat) and place under a moderately hot grill. Grill 5 minutes each side.
3 Towards end of cooking time add the bacon rashers and grill each side 1 minute. Serve both at once.

Fried cod's roe and bacon

you will need:

8 oz. fresh cod's roe	butter OR vegetable shortening for frying
1 small egg, lightly beaten	2–4 bacon rashers
toasted breadcrumbs	½ lemon

1 Place the cod's roe in a saucepan and cover with cold salted water. Bring to the boil and simmer 15 minutes. Drain and cool.
2 Cut cooked roe into ½-inch slices; dip first in lightly beaten egg, and then in toasted breadcrumbs, and coat thoroughly.
3 Fry in hot fat until browned, then push the roes to one side and fry the bacon rashers.
4 Drain and serve with the lemon juice squeezed over the cod's roe.

Grilled tomatoes

you will need:

4 tomatoes	2 slices bread
salt and pepper	
pinch sugar	**to garnish:**
melted butter OR oil for grilling	chopped parsley

1 Slice the tomatoes in halves, season and sprinkle with sugar. Brush each with melted butter or oil, arrange in the base of a grill pan.
2 Place under a moderate heat and grill for 6–8 minutes.
3 Toast the bread and butter.
4 When tomatoes are cooked (the centres should be quite soft), lift carefully on to toast slices, allowing four tomato halves per slice.
5 Serve sprinkled with a little chopped parsley.

Bacon and eggs

you will need:

2 bacon rashers	little butter for frying
2 eggs	

1 Arrange trimmed rashers in a cold frying pan. Fry gently over moderate heat for 3–4 minutes until cooked. Lift from the pan to a warm serving dish.
2 In the remaining fat fry eggs (adding extra butter if required). Crack the eggs one at a time into a cup and add to the hot fat. Tip the pan towards you while adding the egg to prevent the white from spreading.
3 Cook over gentle heat, basting frequently, then lift carefully on to platter and serve with bacon.

Kippered eggs

you will need:

2 kippers	1 oz. butter OR
2 eggs	margarine
2 tablespoons milk	2 slices bread
salt and pepper	
	to garnish:
	chopped parsley

1 Place the kippers in a deep jug and pour over boiling water. Allow to stand for 10 minutes then drain. Flake the flesh, removing any bone and skin.
2 Lightly mix the eggs, milk and seasoning, adding kipper flesh.
3 Heat the butter in a saucepan and stir in the egg mixture. Cook gently until the eggs have thickened.
4 Toast bread and butter.
5 Draw the pan off the heat, spoon the mixture on to the hot buttered toast and serve. Sprinkle with chopped parsley.

Eggs in bacon rings

you will need:

2 rashers bacon	salt and pepper
2 eggs	2 slices bread
½ oz. melted butter OR margarine	

1 Trim the bacon rashers and grill lightly.
2 Butter the bases of two individual baking dishes and line the sides with the bacon rashers.
3 Crack an egg into each dish, add a little melted butter or margarine and season.
4 Place in centre of a moderate oven (355°F. – Gas Mark 4) and bake for 20 minutes or until the egg is set.
5 Toast bread and butter.
6 Loosen the sides of the egg, turn on to toast and serve.

Gammon rashers and apple rings

you will need:

2 thin gammon rashers	1 oz. butter OR
1 eating OR cooking apple (sharp-flavoured)	margarine for frying

1 Trim the rashers. Peel and slice the apple into ¼-inch rings. To keep rings white cover with cold salted water until ready to fry.
2 Fry the rashers over moderate heat for 3–4 minutes in the butter or margarine.
3 Lift out on to a warm serving dish, then add the apple rings to the pan. Arrange so that they all lie flat and then fry gently for 2–3 minutes, turning when browned on the underside – take care not to overcook.
4 Serve the rashers topped with apple rings.

Eggs baked in a dish

you will need:

¼ oz. butter OR	salt and pepper
margarine	2 slices bread
2 eggs	

1 Divide the butter or margarine between two flame-proof individual baking dishes.
2 Place an asbestos or protective mat over heat and set dishes on top. Allow the butter to melt then crack an egg into each dish.
3 Season and cook over a moderate heat until egg is beginning to set.
4 Loosen sides with a knife and turn the egg over in the dish. *continued*

9

5 Toast bread and butter.

6 Remove egg from the heat, turn out on to slices of buttered toast and serve at once.

Herring with bacon

you will need:

2 herrings
little milk
salt and pepper
medium oatmeal for coating

little butter OR margarine for frying
2 rashers bacon
2 tomatoes (optional)

1 Ask the fishmonger to remove the heads and clean the herrings. Place fish on a clean working surface, the inside downwards. Press down the back to loosen the bone, turn over and pull it away.

2 Dip both sides of the boned herrings in seasoned milk and then oatmeal, to coat thoroughly. Pat coating on firmly.

3 Place the fish flesh side down into the hot butter or margarine and cook gently for about 4 minutes. Turn carefully to avoid breaking and cook the second side.

4 Meanwhile trim and grill the bacon rashers. Dish the herrings with the cooked bacon rashers and grilled tomatoes if liked.

Fried sweetbreads and mushrooms

you will need:

8 oz. calf's sweet-breads
¼ pint stock OR water plus stock cube
flour OR beaten egg, browned breadcrumbs for coating

2 oz. butter for frying
2–3 oz. mushrooms, sliced

to garnish:
lemon

1 The day before, soak the sweetbreads in salted water for 1 hour. Rinse and place in a saucepan with cold water to cover. Bring to the boil and drain.

2 Trim away any fat or loose tissue from the sweetbreads and replace in the saucepan, covering with stock.

3 Bring to the boil and simmer gently for ¾–1 hour or until the sweetbreads are tender. Drain and leave to cool overnight pressed between two plates and a heavy weight.

4 Cut the sweetbreads in 1-inch slices, and either coat with flour or dip in beaten egg and breadcrumbs. Fry in the hot butter until browned on both sides. Lift out on to a hot plate and keep warm while frying the mushrooms in the hot butter.

5 Serve the sweetbreads and mushrooms with a wedge of lemon.

When you're out all day

After a day out – whether shopping, working or just enjoying yourself – it is pleasant to come home to a meal that is quick and easy to prepare or, better still, one that is piping hot and ready to serve.

It is possible to plan recipes so that all the lengthy preparation can be done ahead and only a final heating-through is necessary before serving. This should only be done with recipes such as those in this section, where the preparation can be completed in one stage.

If you are lucky enough to have an automatic cooker do put it to good use with the recipes I have given specially for this type of cooker. Additional ideas and information can, of course, be obtained from the manufacturers.

Fish cakes

you will need:

12 oz. cooked mashed potatoes
8 oz. white fish (cod or haddock)
salt and pepper
¼ pint milk

1 tablespoon chopped parsley
1 large egg
toasted breadcrumbs for coating
oil for frying

To prepare ahead

1 Either use cooked leftover potato or boil the required quantity and mash.

2 Cut the fish into pieces and place in a buttered baking or pie dish. Season and add the milk.

3 Cover with a buttered paper, place in the centre of a moderate oven (355°F. – Gas Mark 4) and

bake for 20–25 minutes or until the fish is cooked and flakes easily.

4 Allow the cooked fish to cool a few minutes, then carefully flake the flesh, discarding all skin and bones.

5 Add the fish to the mashed potato with seasoning, parsley and enough of the lightly beaten egg to blend the mixture together.

6 Turn out on to a clean working surface and divide into four portions. With floured hands, shape into four neat patties.

7 Pour the remainder of the beaten egg into a shallow dish and dip the patties first into the egg, coating both sides, and then into the breadcrumbs. Pat the coating on firmly and set aside in a cold place.

About 20 minutes before serving

Fry the fish cakes over moderate heat in the hot oil until golden brown. Allow about 5 minutes each side, turning frequently to get even browning. Drain and serve with grilled tomatoes and green peas.

Tuna pasties

you will need:

1 7-oz. tin tuna fish	1 teaspoon lemon juice
salt and pepper	1 egg, lightly mixed
1 tablespoon chopped parsley	8 oz. frozen puff pastry, thawed
pinch curry powder	
1 tablespoon fresh white breadcrumbs	

To prepare ahead

1 Drain the tuna fish and flake the flesh into a basin. Add seasoning, parsley, curry powder, breadcrumbs, lemon juice and enough egg to bind to a moist consistency.

2 On a lightly floured working surface, roll the pastry out thinly to a 10-inch square. Trim the edges and then cut into four smaller squares.

3 Spoon a quarter of the filling into the centre of each portion of pastry.

4 Damp edges and fold pastry over to make a triangular shape. Press edges together to seal, then slash pastry top. Store in refrigerator.

About 35 minutes before serving

Place the pasties on a wet baking tray. Brush over with remaining beaten egg mixed with a little milk and place above centre in a hot oven (425°F. – Gas Mark 7). Bake 10 minutes, then lower the heat to (380°F. – Gas Mark 5) and bake a further 20 minutes.

Old-fashioned fish pie

you will need:

8 oz. white fish – use haddock or cod fillet	1 oz. butter OR margarine
¼ pint milk	1 tablespoon flour
8 oz. (3 medium) potatoes for the topping	1 tablespoon finely chopped parsley
	salt and pepper

To prepare ahead

1 Place the fish in a greased pie dish and add the milk. Cover with a buttered paper, place in the centre of a very moderate oven (355°F. – Gas Mark 4) and bake 15 minutes or until fish is cooked and the flesh flakes.

2 Meanwhile boil the potatoes. Lift the fish from the liquor, reserving this for the sauce. Bone and flake the fish flesh and set aside.

3 Melt the butter or margarine in a saucepan and stir in the flour. Cook gently for 1 minute but do not brown.

4 Gradually stir in the milk (make up to ⅓ pint if necessary with extra milk), and beat thoroughly to get a really smooth sauce. Bring to the boil and cook gently for 2–3 minutes.

5 Add the chopped parsley and the cooked flaked fish. Pour into a greased 1½-pint pie or baking dish.

6 Top with the potatoes mashed with salt, pepper and a little butter, and rough the surface up with a fork.

Variations

With tomato – add chopped tomato flesh, instead of parsley.
With egg – add sliced hard-boiled egg instead of parsley.

About 40 minutes before serving

Place high in a moderate oven (355°F. – Gas Mark 4) and bake until heated through and the top well browned (about 30–35 minutes). Serve with green peas.

Mince and potato pie

you will need:

½ small onion, chopped finely	1 teaspoon salt
½ oz. lard OR dripping	pinch pepper
6–8 oz. minced beef	8 oz. (about 3 medium) potatoes
½ tin cream of oxtail soup	

To prepare ahead

1 Fry the onion in hot fat for about 5 minutes to soften. Add the beef and brown.

2 Stir in the oxtail soup, season and bring up to the boil. *continued*

3 Pour into a buttered 1-pint pie dish or baking dish.

4 Boil the potatoes, then mash with a fork and add seasoning, butter and milk, beating until smooth and creamy.

5 Fork mixture over the top of the meat.

About 45 minutes before serving

Place in the centre of a hot oven (380°F. – Gas Mark 5) and bake 40 minutes. Serve at once with grilled tomatoes or green peas.

Cottage pie

you will need:

½ oz. lard OR dripping	¼ pint stock OR water
8 oz. minced beef	plus stock cube
1 small onion, finely chopped	**for the topping:**
1 teaspoon salt	12 oz.–1 lb. potatoes
pinch pepper	1 tablespoon milk
1 teaspoon tomato purée	½ oz. butter

To prepare ahead

1 Heat the lard or dripping and add the minced beef. Fry over moderate heat until browned.

2 Add the onion, seasoning, tomato purée and stock and bring to the boil. Lower the heat and simmer gently for 30 minutes, covered with a lid.

3 Pour the mixture into the base of a 1½-pint pie or baking dish and set aside while preparing the potato topping.

4 Boil the potatoes. Mash with plenty of seasoning, then beat in the milk until creamy and smooth.

5 Fork potato mixture over the minced beef and dot the surface with butter.

About 40 minutes before serving

Place the pie in the centre of a moderate oven (355°F. – Gas Mark 4) and allow to heat through for about 35 minutes, until contents are hot and top is browned. Serve with green beans.

Mince and potato patties

you will need:

2 oz. butter OR margarine	stock OR water plus stock cube
1 medium onion, chopped	pinch mixed herbs
4 oz. minced beef	12 oz. potatoes
1 teaspoon flour	1 egg, lightly mixed
salt and pepper	toasted breadcrumbs for coating

To prepare ahead

1 Heat half the butter and fry the onion until soft (about 5 minutes). Stir in the minced beef and brown quickly.

2 Season, stir in the flour, and then sufficient water or stock to cover. Add the mixed herbs.

Bring to the boil, lower the heat and cover. Simmer gently for 20 minutes.

3 Pour into a basin and set aside until quite cold.

4 Boil and mash the potatoes with plenty of seasoning. Add half the mixed egg and beat until creamy and smooth. Turn out on to a lightly floured working surface and divide the mixture into 4 portions.

5 Shape each one into a ball and hollow out the centre. Spoon the mince into this, draw the potato over the top, turn over and pat into a neat patty shape with floured fingers.

6 Dip the patties first in remaining beaten egg and then in toasted breadcrumbs. Store in a refrigerator.

About 15 minutes before serving

Fry in remaining butter or margarine, turning once until golden brown and crisp.

Potato Scotch eggs

you will need:

8–12 oz. potatoes	3 eggs
salt and pepper	toasted breadcrumbs for coating
1 teaspoon finely chopped parsley or chives	deep fat for frying
	4 bacon rashers

To prepare ahead

1 Boil and mash the potatoes. Season well and add the parsley or chives.

2 Turn the mixture out on to a lightly floured working surface and divide into 2 portions.

3 Meanwhile hard-boil 2 of the eggs, plunge into cold water and remove the shells. Coat each egg with a portion of potato.

4 Crack the remaining egg into a shallow dish and season. Mix lightly and coat each potato-coated egg first with beaten egg and then with toasted breadcrumbs. Coat thoroughly, then refrigerate until ready to serve.

About 10 minutes before serving

Fry in hot deep fat for 6–8 minutes, until golden brown and heated through. Drain and serve, sliced in half, with the grilled bacon rashers.

Lamb chop casserole

you will need:

2 lamb chops	2 rounded teaspoons flour
salt and pepper	½ pint water
1 onion, sliced	
1 rounded teaspoon gravy thickening powder	

To prepare ahead

1 Trim the chops and season lightly; place in a

greased ovenproof casserole and cover with the onion.

2 In a small basin blend together the gravy thickening powder and flour with enough of the cold water to make a thin paste.
3 Bring the remaining water to the boil and pour on to the mixture, stirring well. Return to the saucepan and bring to the boil, stirring well all the time, until thickened.
4 Pour this gravy over the contents of the casserole dish. Cool, cover and store in refrigerator.

About 1 hour before serving

Cover with a lid and place in the centre of a moderate oven (355°F. – Gas Mark 4) and bake for 1 hour. Serve with buttered carrots.

Gammon steaks with pineapple

using oven time control

you will need:

2 gammon steaks, ¼-½-inch thick	pineapple juice from tin
2 tinned pineapple rings	

To prepare ahead

1 Remove the rind from the gammon rashers and snip the fat at ½-inch intervals to help prevent buckling during cooking.
2 Place the rashers in a casserole dish and top each with a pineapple ring. Add 2–3 tablespoons of juice from the tin.
3 Cover with a lid and place in the centre of the oven. *Set oven temperature at very moderate (355°F. – Gas Mark 4) and set time control for 1 hour.*
4 Serve the rashers with pineapple rings and a little juice from the dish.

Bacon and onion dumplings

using oven time control

you will need:

	for the pastry:
2 large onions	4 oz. plain flour
4 rashers back bacon	pinch salt
salt and pepper	2 oz. butter OR margarine
	1 oz. grated Cheddar cheese
	water to mix

Early in the day

1 Place whole, peeled onions in a saucepan, cover with cold water and bring up to the boil. Lower the heat and simmer slowly for 30 minutes or until tender.

2 Drain onions and, keeping whole, carefully remove the centres. Chop or mince centres along with the trimmed bacon rashers and season well.
3 Spoon the filling back into the onion centres and set aside while preparing the pastry.
4 Sift the flour and salt into a basin. Rub in the fat and add the cheese. Stir in enough water to mix to a firm dough. Turn out on to a lightly floured working surface and knead lightly.
5 Roll out very thinly and, using a saucer as a guide, cut out 2 circles of pastry. Reserve the trimmings.
6 Place an onion in the centre of each piece of pastry, damp the edges and draw the pastry up to cover the onion. Pinch the edges together to seal, turn over and place sealed edges downwards on a greased baking tray. Decorate the tops with any left-over pieces of pastry, and brush the dumplings with a little milk.
7 Place in the centre of the oven. *Set oven temperature to hot (400°F. – Gas Mark 6) and the control for 40 minutes.*
8 Serve hot with gravy and green beans.

Bacon and onion crumble

using oven time control

you will need:

	for the topping:
4 oz. back bacon rashers	4 oz. plain flour
1 large onion	salt and pepper
4 oz. mushrooms	2 oz. butter OR margarine
4 oz. tomatoes	2 oz. cheese, grated
salt and pepper	
4 tablespoons water	
1 oz. butter OR margarine	

To prepare ahead

1 Trim the rind and cut the bacon rashers in halves. Peel and slice the onion and the mushrooms (including the stems), and slice the tomatoes.
2 Arrange the ingredients in layers in a buttered 1½–2 pint casserole dish, seasoning each layer well. Pour on the water.
3 Prepare the topping. Sieve the flour and seasoning together. Rub in the margarine, and stir in the cheese. Sprinkle the crumble topping over the contents of the casserole and press down lightly.
4 Place in the centre of the oven. *Set oven to moderately hot (380°F. – Gas Mark 5) and the control for 1½ hours.*
5 Serve with green peas or beans.

Frankfurter and corn bake

using oven time control

you will need:

2 eggs
1 7-oz. tin cream style
sweet corn
2 heaped tablespoons
fresh white bread-
crumbs
½ onion, finely chopped

pinch dry mustard
salt and pepper
4 frankfurter sausages

to garnish:
chopped parsley

Early in the day

1 Lightly whisk the eggs in a basin; add the sweet corn, breadcrumbs, onion, mustard, seasoning and mix well.
2 Cut the frankfurters into ½-inch lengths and stir into the mixture.
3 Pour into a well-greased shallow 1½-pint pie or baking dish and place in the centre of the oven. *Set the oven temperature to moderately hot (380°F. – Gas Mark 5) and time control for 40–50 minutes' cooking time.*
4 Remove from the heat, sprinkle with chopped parsley and serve.

Lamb and kidney casserole

you will need:

1 lb. middle neck of
lamb
2 lamb's kidneys
seasoned flour
1 oz. lard OR dripping
1 carrot, sliced

1 onion, sliced
¾ pint stock OR water
plus stock cube
salt and pepper
3 medium potatoes

To prepare ahead

1 Wipe the meat, separate the pieces and trim away any excess fat. Remove any fat from around the kidneys and slice in halves. Snip out the core.
2 Toss the meat and kidneys in seasoned flour then fry in hot lard or dripping until browned.
3 Arrange the prepared vegetables in the base of a fireproof dish. Place the browned meat and kidneys on top. Add a little seasoned flour to the hot fat in the pan and cook for a few minutes until bubbling and brown.
4 Gradually stir in the hot stock, bring to the boil and season.
5 Peel and slice the potatoes and arrange neatly over the top of the casserole dish. Strain over the gravy. Cover with buttered papers and a lid and store in refrigerator.

About 1 hour 35 minutes before serving

Place in the centre of a slow oven (335°F. – Gas Mark 3) and cook 1½ hours. Remove the lid and papers about 20 minutes before the end of the cooking time to allow for browning.

Corned beef hamburger

you will need:

4 oz. corned beef
4 oz. cooked mashed
potato
2 tablespoons fresh
white breadcrumbs
pinch of mixed herbs

salt and pepper
1 tablespoon table
sauce for meat
1 egg, lightly beaten
flour for coating

To prepare ahead

1 Measure the corned beef, mashed potato, breadcrumbs, mixed herbs and plenty of seasoning into a basin.
2 Add the sauce and enough lightly beaten egg to bind the mixture together.
3 Turn out on to a lightly floured working surface and divide the mixture into 4 portions. With floured fingers shape each portion into a patty, and flour lightly. Store in a refrigerator.

About 30 minutes before serving

Arrange on a well-greased baking tray and place in the centre of a moderate oven (355°F. – Gas Mark 4) and bake for 30 minutes or until crisp and browned, turning the patties once.
Serve with grilled tomatoes and fried bacon rashers.

Braised lambs' hearts

using oven time control

you will need:

2 lambs' hearts
seasoned flour
1 oz. dripping OR
vegetable shortening
2 large carrots, sliced
1 onion, sliced
1 pint stock
2 level teaspoons corn-
flour

for the stuffing:

¼ small onion, finely
chopped
½ oz. margarine
2 heaped tablespoons
fresh white bread-
crumbs
1 tablespoon shredded
beef suet
1 teaspoon chopped
parsley
pinch mixed herbs
salt and pepper
lightly mixed egg

Early in the day

1 Soak the lambs' hearts in salted water for 30 minutes. Cut away any coarse pipes and valves, using a pair of scissors, and trim off surplus fat. Set aside while preparing the stuffing.
2 Sauté the onion gently in the hot fat for 5 minutes until soft. Draw the pan off the heat and, using a fork, stir in the breadcrumbs, suet, parsley, mixed herbs and a seasoning of salt and pepper.
3 Stir in enough lightly beaten egg to make a moist consistency. Pack the stuffing into the prepared hearts then, using a large needle and coarse thread, sew across the tops of the hearts to close.

4 Roll the hearts in seasoned flour and brown in the hot dripping. Lift from the pan, place in a casserole over a base of prepared vegetables, and add the stock.

5 Cover with a lid and place in the centre of the oven. *Set the oven temperature at slow (335°F. – Gas Mark 3) and the time control for 2 hours.*

6 Lift the hearts from the casserole and remove the thread. Strain the cooking liquor, and reserve ½ pint.

7 In a small basin blend the cornflour with a little cold water to a thin paste, and stir into the stock. Strain back into a saucepan, and bring to the boil, stirring all the time. Check the seasoning.

8 Serve the hearts with gravy, vegetables and creamed potatoes.

Carbonnade of beef

using oven time control

you will need:

12 oz. beef skirt	3 onions, sliced
seasoned flour	½ pint stock OR vege-
1 oz. lard OR dripping	table cooking water

1 Trim away any fat from the meat. Using a sharp knife and holding it at an angle, cut the meat into thin slices. Toss these in seasoned flour and fry in the hot fat until brown on both sides.

2 Drain the meat from the pan and arrange in a casserole dish in layers with the prepared onions.

3 Meanwhile add a little extra flour to the frying pan and stir over moderate heat until browned. Stir in the stock and bring to the boil.

4 Strain over the meat and onion, cover with a lid and place in the centre of the oven. *Set oven to slow (310°F. – Gas Mark 2) and time control for 2½ hours.*

5 Serve with buttered carrots and boiled potatoes.

Lancashire hot pot

using oven time control

you will need:

1 lb. scrag end of	1 level **teaspoon salt,**
middle neck of mutton	and pinch of pepper
seasoned flour	½ pint stock or vege-
8 oz. potatoes	table cooking water
6 carrots	
1 large onion	**to garnish:**
1 stalk celery	chopped parsley
½ level teaspoon mixed	
herbs	

1 Trim away the fat, gristle or bone from the meat and then cut into cubes and roll in seasoned flour. Fry in hot fat to seal and brown lightly.

2 Slice the potatoes, reserving about half the best slices for the top. Arrange remainder in the base of a casserole dish.

3 Slice the carrots and onion. Wash, trim and slice the celery. Toss them with the mixed herbs and seasoning.

4 Arrange alternate layers of mixed vegetables and meat over the potato slices in the casserole. Top with reserved potato slices, neatly arranged, and pour over the stock. Cover with a greased paper and a lid.

5 Place in the centre of the oven. *Set oven temperature to slow (335°F. – Gas Mark 3) and the control for 2–3½ hours.*

6 If possible, half an hour before serving remove the lid and paper from the casserole. Brush the potatoes with a little fat and sprinkle lightly with salt. Replace the casserole near the top of the oven without a lid and allow the potatoes to crisp. Sprinkle with chopped parsley and serve.

Spanish chicken

you will need:

2 chicken joints	½ pint stock OR water
salt and pepper	plus chicken stock
2 tablespoons cooking	cube
oil	1 8-oz. tin tomatoes
1 onion, chopped	1 small packet frozen
6 oz. long grain rice	peas

To prepare ahead

1 Trim the chicken joints and season with salt and pepper.

2 Fry in the hot oil to brown quickly, and then lower the heat and cook for 15 minutes, turning occasionally.

3 Transfer the joints to a casserole dish and add the onion to the hot fat. Fry gently for 5 minutes until soft, then stir in the rice.

4 Add the stock and tomatoes plus liquid from the pan. Bring to the boil, stir and pour over the chicken joints. Cool and place in refrigerator.

About 40 minutes before serving

Place the casserole in the centre of a very moderate oven (335°F. – Gas Mark 4) and cook 40 minutes. About 10 minutes before cooking time is completed, stir in the peas. Re-cover and leave to cook until the rice is tender and liquid absorbed.

Egg croquettes

you will need:

1½ oz. butter OR	dash Worcestershire
margarine	sauce
1½ oz. flour	2 hard-boiled eggs
¼ pint milk	4 rashers streaky bacon
4 oz. grated Cheddar	lightly beaten egg
cheese	brown breadcrumbs
salt and pepper	fat for frying

To prepare ahead

1 Melt the butter or margarine over low heat and *continued*

stir in the flour. Gradually beat in the milk and bring to the boil. The mixture will be very thick at this stage.

2 Add the cheese and stir over heat until melted, season and add the Worcestershire sauce.

3 Draw the pan off the heat and add the chopped hard-boiled eggs.

4 Spread the mixture to ½-inch thickness on a plate and leave until quite cold.

5 Divide into four portions, roll each into a fat croquette shape and wrap each in a bacon rasher. Dip first in lightly beaten egg and then browned crumbs. Refrigerate until ready to cook.

About 10 minutes before serving

Fry in deep hot fat until golden brown (about 6 minutes). Drain on absorbent paper and serve with extra bacon rashers and grilled tomatoes.

Swiss steak with vegetables

you will need:

12 oz.–1 lb. braising steak	8 oz. carrots, sliced
seasoned flour	¼ pint stock OR water plus stock cube
½ oz. dripping	1 small packet frozen peas, thawed
1 onion, chopped	

To prepare ahead

1 Trim away any fat and gristle from the meat and cut into 4 pieces. Roll the meat in seasoned flour. Fry in the hot dripping to brown quickly.

2 Place the prepared vegetables in the base of a casserole dish and arrange the browned meat on top. Add the stock and cover with a lid.

3 Place in the centre of a slow oven (335°F. – Gas Mark 3) and cook for 1½ hours. Cool and store in refrigerator.

About 30 minutes before serving

Stir in the peas and then place in the centre of a moderate oven (355°F. – Gas Mark 4) and cook for further half hour.

Sausage and tomato casserole

using oven time control

you will need:

8 oz. beef chipolatas	¼ pint stock OR water plus stock cube
½ oz. dripping	
1 onion, sliced	1 rounded teaspoon cornflour
1 8-oz. tin tomatoes	
salt and pepper	

1 Separate the sausages and quickly fry in the hot dripping to brown. Lift from the pan and place the sausages in the base of a casserole dish.

2 Add the onion to the hot fat and cook gently for 5 minutes until brown. Add to the sausages with the tomatoes and liquid from the tin, a seasoning of salt and pepper and the stock.

3 Cover with a lid and place in the centre of the oven. *Set oven temperature to moderate (355°F. – Gas Mark 4) and time control for 1 hour cooking time.*

4 Lift the cooked sausages from the casserole on to a hot serving dish. Sieve the sauce into a saucepan and stir in the cornflour, blended with a little water to a smooth paste. Re-heat, stirring until boiling, check the seasoning and pour over the sausages.

Casseroled turnips or parsnips

using oven time control

you will need:

8–12 oz. turnip or parsnip	½ oz. butter
	2–3 tablespoons stock
salt and pepper	OR water

1 Peel and cut the vegetables into suitable sized small pieces. Place in a casserole or baking dish and season well.

2 Add the butter and stock or water. Cover with a lid and place in the centre of the oven. *Set oven temperature at moderately hot (380°F. – Gas Mark 5) and set time control for 1 hour.*

3 Remove lid and serve the parsnips or turnip along with a little juice from the dish.

Baked onions

you will need:

4 small onions	2–3 tablespoons stock
½ oz. butter	OR water
	salt

1 Place peeled, whole onions in a saucepan and cover with cold water. Bring up to the boil slowly, then drain.

2 Place in a casserole or baking dish along with the butter and stock or water.

3 Cover with a lid and place in the centre of the oven. *Set oven temperature to moderately hot (380°F. – Gas Mark 5) and set time control for 1 hour.*

4 Remove the lid, drain the onions, sprinkle with salt and serve.

French or runner beans

using oven time control

you will need:

8–12 oz. runner OR French beans	pinch salt
	2–3 tablespoons stock OR water

1 Wash the beans, string and slice with a sharp

knife. Place in a fireproof casserole or baking dish and sprinkle with salt. Add sufficient stock or water to cover the base of the dish.

2 Cover with a lid and place in the centre of the oven. *Set oven temperature to moderately hot (380°F. – Gas Mark 5) and set time control for 45 minutes.*

3 Serve the beans drained from juices in the dish.

Ham gnocchi

you will need:

½ pint milk	3 oz. grated Parmesan
¼ level teaspoon salt	OR Cheddar cheese
freshly ground black	2 oz. butter
pepper	¼ level teaspoon made
2 oz. fine semolina	mustard
2 oz. chopped ham	1 egg, well beaten
1 teaspoon chopped	
parsley	

To prepare ahead

1 Heat the milk with the salt and pepper. Sprinkle in the semolina and bring to the boil, stirring. Cook gently for about 3 minutes, until the mixture thickens. Stir in the chopped ham and parsley.

2 Draw the pan off the heat and stir in 2 oz. of the cheese, 1½ oz. of butter, and the mustard. Beat in the egg and stir over a low heat for 1 minute, without boiling.

3 Turn the mixture out on to a greased shallow plate, spreading about ½ inch thick. Leave until quite cold. Using a wetted cutter (or the rim of a glass tumbler) cut the mixture into rounds and arrange overlapping in a greased shallow baking dish.

4 Top with remaining cheese and dot with remaining butter. Refrigerate and leave until ready to serve.

About half an hour before serving

Set the oven at moderately hot (380°F. – Gas Mark 5). Place the gnocchi in the centre and heat through for 20–25 minutes, until hot and golden brown. Serve with tomato salad and hot buttered toast.

Baked tomatoes

using oven time control

you will need:

4 tomatoes	½ oz. butter
salt and pepper	2–3 tablespoons stock
little chopped parsley	OR water
OR chives	

1 Plunge the tomatoes into boiling water for 1 minute. Drain and peel away the skins.

2 Place the tomatoes in a fireproof casserole or baking dish and sprinkle with seasoning. Add a little parsley or chives, the butter and sufficient stock or water to cover the base of the dish.

3 Cover with a buttered paper and a lid and place in the centre of the oven. *Set oven to moderately hot (380°F. – Gas Mark 5) and set time control for 35 minutes cooking time.*

4 Remove lid and buttered paper and serve tomatoes with a little juice from the dish.

Oven-cooked carrots

using oven time control

you will need:

8 oz. carrots	2–3 tablespoons stock
salt and pepper	OR water
pinch sugar	
½ oz. butter	**to decorate:**
	chopped parsley

1 Place thinly sliced carrots in a casserole or baking dish, season well, add the sugar, butter and sufficient stock to cover the base of the dish.

2 Cover with a lid and place in the centre of the oven. *Set oven to moderately hot (380°F. – Gas Mark 5) and set time control for 1 hour cooking time.*

3 Serve the carrots sprinkled with parsley and juices from the dish.

Casseroling fruits, with oven time control

All fruits suitable for stewing can be cooked in a casserole, although apples and pears do tend to discolour. This method is ideal with an automatic cooker.

Fresh fruit

Prepare 8 oz. fresh fruit, according to kind chosen, and place in a casserole dish. Pour over a sugar syrup made up as follows. Dissolve 1–2 oz. castor sugar in ¼ pint water (allow ½ pint for hard fruits), and bring to the boil. Pour over the fruit, cover casserole and place in the centre of the oven. *Set oven temperature to slow (335°F. – Gas Mark 3) and time control for ½–1 hour,* according to fruit chosen.

Dried fruit

Wash the fruit and place in the casserole dish. Cover with 1 pint water and leave to soak for at least 12 hours. Add 2–3 oz. castor sugar and cook as above.

Banana bake

using oven time control

you will need:

1 large banana	**for the topping:**
1 dessertspoon clear honey	1½ oz. self-raising flour
	1 level tablespoon cocoa powder
	1 oz. shredded beef suet
	1½ oz. castor sugar
	milk to mix

1 Peel and slice the banana and place in the base of a buttered ½–1 pint pie dish. Drizzle the honey over the banana.
2 To make the topping, sift together the flour and cocoa powder into a basin. Add the suet and sugar and stir in enough milk to mix to a medium soft consistency.
3 Spoon the mixture over the banana base and spread evenly.
4 Place in the centre of the oven. *Set oven to very moderate (355°F. – Gas Mark 4) and time control for 30 minutes.*
5 Serve hot with cream or top of the milk.

Apple shortbread crumble

using oven time control

you will need:

2 sharp-flavoured apples	**for the shortbread crumble:**
1 tablespoon water	2 oz. plain flour
½ oz. butter	1 oz. butter OR margarine
1 oz. castor sugar	1 tablespoon castor sugar

1 Peel, core and slice the apples into a saucepan. Add the water and butter, cover and cook gently, stirring occasionally until the apple is quite soft.
2 Stir in the sugar and spoon the mixture into the base of a 1-pint baking or pie dish. Set aside to cool while preparing the crumble topping.
3 Sift the flour into a basin and rub in the butter or margarine. Add the sugar and continue to rub in until the mixture clings together in small lumps.
4 Spoon the crumble mixture over the apple and pack down lightly. Place in the centre of the oven. *Set oven temperature to very moderate (355°F. – Gas Mark 4) and time control for 30 minutes.*
5 Serve hot with cream or ice cream.

Two-way dishes for weekends

I must confess that although I really do enjoy cooking, during most weekends I want to be free to relax, or go out and visit friends. So here are the recipes which I find are a most suitable choice for a weekend when I want to spend as little time as possible in the kitchen. You'll notice that most recipes are deliberately planned to provide for a second meal. Some may find it an advantage to cook the joint on Saturday and use the second recipe for Sunday lunch or, alternatively, to cook the joint for Sunday lunch and serve the second recipe for Sunday supper. Either way, take advantage of these dual-purpose recipes and cut down on kitchen time.

A joint for two

There is no need to avoid joints simply because there are only two of you. A roast can be an economical buy for a weekend, as long as you make use of the leftover meat. For ideas see the suggestions in this section, or turn to page 56. Ask your butcher for advice about the best meat for small joints, from 1½ lb.–2 lb., depending on the cut.

To make gravy for a roast meal
Pour off the hot fat from the tin very slowly so that all the sediment and meat juices stay in the pan. Place over low heat in cooker top.
For thin gravy – add a dash of salt and pepper and stir in about 1 pint stock or vegetable cooking water. Stir and boil briskly till reduced by about half. Taste and correct seasoning and strain into a hot gravy boat.
For thick gravy – leave 1 tablespoon of fat in the tin and stir in 1 tablespoon flour. Cook 1 minute until bubbling and frothy, then draw the tin off the heat and stir in about ½ pint stock or vegetable cooking water. Replace over the heat and bring to the boil, stirring well and cook for 2–3

minutes. Taste to check seasoning, add a little gravy browning if liked, then strain into a hot gravy boat and serve.

Yorkshire pudding

| 2 oz. plain flour | 1 egg |
| pinch salt | ¼ pint milk |

1 Sieve the flour and salt into a basin and hollow out the centre.
2 Add egg and half milk and gradually beat into the flour drawing the mixture in from the sides of the basin. Beat until smooth, add remaining milk and beat thoroughly to aerate.
3 Set aside to stand for 1 hour.
4 Preheat the oven for 15 minutes (425°F. – Gas Mark 7). Using a special Yorkshire pudding tin with four separate sections, place a nut of dripping in each one. Put in the oven until the fat is thoroughly hot, add the batter and replace immediately on the top shelf.
5 Bake for 20 minutes or until risen and crisp. Serve at once.

Winter casserole and Bacon patties

you will need:

1 lb. piece collar bacon	1 15-oz. tin tomatoes
1 oz. lard OR vegetable shortening	1 bay leaf
1 onion, sliced	1 tablespoon flour
8 oz. carrots, sliced	½ pint stock OR water plus stock cube
½ swede, peeled and cut in cubes	salt and pepper

First meal

1 Soak the bacon joint in cold water for 3–4 hours. Strip the rind, remove excess fat and cut the bacon into cubes.
2 Melt the dripping in a pan and brown the bacon pieces, then remove from the fat.
3 Add the prepared root vegetables to the hot fat and fry gently for 4–5 minutes. Drain the vegetables and put into a casserole with the bacon, adding the tomatoes plus liquid from the tin, and the bay leaf.
4 Sprinkle the flour over the hot fat in the pan and cook for 1 minute. Gradually stir in the stock and bring to the boil. Strain over the contents of the casserole dish.
5 Cover with a lid and place in the centre of a moderate oven (355°F. – Gas Mark 4) and cook for 2–2½ hours.
6 Remove the bay leaf, check the seasoning and serve with creamed potatoes.

Second meal

for the patties:	beaten egg
cooked mashed potato	toasted breadcrumbs
leftover bacon	to coat
made mustard	fat for frying
seasoning	
dash Worcestershire sauce	

For the bacon patties, combine equal quantities of cooked mashed potato and minced bacon. Season well with salt and pepper and add a little made mustard and a dash of Worcestershire sauce to taste. Shape into neat round patties and dip first in beaten egg and then in toasted breadcrumbs. Fry in hot fat until crisp and golden brown on both sides. Serve with grilled tomatoes.

Braised brisket of beef and Cooked-meat curry

you will need:

1 small piece (1½–2 lb.) brisket of beef	*bouquet garni*
	salt and pepper
seasoned flour	½ pint stock OR water plus stock cube
1 onion	1 level tablespoon corn-flour, blended with water to a smooth paste
8 oz. carrots	
½ turnip	
1 oz. dripping	

First meal

1 Check that the meat is neatly tied, skewering if necessary. Dip in seasoned flour and set aside while preparing the vegetables.
2 Peel and slice the onion; scrape and peel thick part from turnip; scrape carrots. Cut the carrots and turnips into thin sticks, then into ½-inch lengths, make neat shapes for serving.
3 Heat the dripping in a large saucepan, brown the meat, then remove from the pan and add the prepared vegetables. Heat gently but do not brown, and place the meat on top.
4 Add the *bouquet garni*, the seasoning and enough stock to cover the vegetables.
5 Bring to boil and simmer 1½–2 hours.
6 Remove the meat, surround with cooked vegetables.
7 Stir the blended cornflour into the strained stock and heat, stirring until boiling and thickened. Strain, then serve with meat and creamed potatoes.

Second meal

For the curry, prepare a curry sauce as on page 54 (curried beef) and simmer for 30 minutes. Cut the left over meat into suitably-sized pieces, and then add to sauce. Heat through for 15 minutes, then serve with plain boiled rice and mango chutney.

Roast lamb and Sliced lamb in gravy

you will need:

1 piece best end neck of lamb (about 1½ lb.) salt and pepper	**for the stuffing:** ½ oz. butter OR margarine 1 small onion, chopped 2 bacon rashers 8 oz. beef sausage meat seasoning

First meal

1 Ask the butcher to bone the joint without rolling. Season and set aside while preparing the stuffing.
2 Melt the butter or margarine over low heat and add the onion. Cook gently until the onion is soft, then add the bacon, trimmed and chopped, and fry for a further 2–3 minutes.
3 Add the butter, onion and bacon to the sausage meat with salt and pepper and mix well.
4 Spread the stuffing over the surface of the lamb and roll up. Tie in several places with string.
5 Put in roasting tin with dripping and place in the centre of a hot oven (400°F. – Gas Mark 6) for 10 minutes to seal, then lower to moderate (355°F. – Gas Mark 4) and roast for a further 50 minutes.
6 Serve sliced, with gravy (see page 18), roast potatoes and broccoli spears.

Second meal

for the sliced lamb in gravy: 1 onion ½ oz. butter 1 level tablespoon flour	½ pint stock OR water and stock cube salt and pepper leftover sliced lamb

For the sliced lamb in gravy, finely chop the onion and fry in butter until soft. Stir in 1 level tablespoon flour and continue to cook until frothy and brown. Gradually stir in ½ pint stock and bring to the boil. Season and add the sliced leftover meat. Cover with a lid and re-heat gently for 15 minutes. Serve with creamed potato and green beans.

Variation

Raisin stuffing for lamb

you will need:

1 cooking apple 4 oz. seedless raisins 1 tablespoon chutney	2 oz. fresh white breadcrumbs salt and pepper 1 egg

1 Peel, core and chop the apple. Mix with the raisins, chutney (chopping large pieces), breadcrumbs and seasoning.
2 Stir in enough lightly mixed egg to bind the mixture together. Use instead of stuffing above.

Pot roast belly of pork and Pork fritters with apple rings

you will need:

1½ lb. piece belly of pork salt and pepper ¼ teaspoon powdered sage 1 oz. dripping OR lard 2–3 onions, halved 8 oz. sharp-flavoured apples, peeled and halved	pinch sugar nut butter **for the gravy:** ½ oz. flour stock OR water plus stock cube seasoning

First meal

1 Wipe the meat, remove any bone, and season with salt, pepper and sage. Either roll the joint and tie securely, or score the skin and leave un-rolled.
2 Heat the dripping in a large heavy pan and place in the joint, skin side up; for crisp crackling, rub a little salt into the skin and do not turn while cooking.
3 Add the onion and apples and cover with a tight-fitting lid. Cook over gentle heat for 1½ hours. Remove lid for last 30 minutes to crispen.
4 Lift cooked joint out and keep warm. Rub apples and onion through a sieve to make a purée, add pinch of sugar and a nut of butter.
5 Prepare a thin gravy with fat and flour, as page 18.
6 Season the gravy, strain and serve with the sliced pork, apple sauce, roast potatoes and braised celery.

Second meal

for pork fritters: slices of leftover pork 1 egg	breadcrumbs to coat 1 apple, cut into rings

For the pork fritters, dip slices of leftover roast pork first in lightly beaten egg, then in brown breadcrumbs, and fry in hot dripping until golden brown, turning to brown evenly. Serve with fried apple rings and sauté potatoes.

Roast loin of pork with sage and onion stuffing, hot and cold

you will need:

1 small loin of pork seasoned flour 1 oz. lard OR dripping **for the stuffing:** 1 medium onion 2½ oz. fresh white breadcrumbs	1 level teaspoon powdered sage ½ level teaspoon salt ¼ level teaspoon pepper 1 oz. butter OR margarine

First meal

1 Cut the loin into the centre lengthwise – *do not cut completely through.* Beat out flat with a

wetted rolling pin. Season and set aside while preparing the stuffing.

2 Peel and cut the onion in half. Place in a pan, cover with cold water, bring to the boil and cook until tender – takes about 20–30 minutes.

3 Drain the cooked onion, chop finely and add to the breadcrumbs, sage and seasoning in a basin. Stir in the melted butter with a fork.

4 Press the stuffing over the pork and roll up from one end. Tie tightly with string in several places.

5 Roll in seasoned flour and then brown in the hot lard or dripping. Place in the centre of a moderate oven (355°F. – Gas Mark 4) and roast for 1 hour 15 minutes.

6 Serve sliced, with roast potatoes and braised celery.

Second meal

Any leftover meat is delicious served cold, sliced, with potato salad, sliced cooked beetroot and chutney.

Devon pie, hot and cold

you will need:

8 oz. short crust pastry (see page 4)	1 onion, finely chopped
	1 carrot, sliced
	pinch mixed herbs
for the filling:	1 egg
8 oz. minced beef	milk to glaze
½ level teaspoon salt	

First meal

1 Butter a 7-inch sponge sandwich tin. On a lightly floured surface roll out half the pastry to a circle just a little larger all round than the tin. Line the tin with pastry, and set aside while preparing the filling.

2 In a basin combine the minced beef, salt, onion, carrot, mixed herbs and egg. Spoon into the pastry-lined tin and spread the mixture evenly. Damp the pastry rim.

3 Roll remaining pastry into a circle to cover the pie. Press round the edges to seal and snip a hole in the centre. Any pastry trimmings can be re-rolled and used to make a decoration of leaves on the pie top.

4 Brush the pie with a little milk and place above centre in a hot oven (400°F. – Gas Mark 6) and bake for 10 minutes, then lower the heat to moderate (355°F. – Gas Mark 4) and bake for a further 40 minutes.

5 Remove from the oven and allow to cool for 5 minutes, then turn out of the tin. Serve half of pie cut in quarters, with grilled mushrooms and green peas.

Second meal

Serve the remaining pie with sliced tomato and onion marinated in French dressing, Russian salad and tossed lettuce.

Lamb soubise and Stovies

you will need:

2 lb. best end of neck of lamb	2 carrots, chopped
	½ pint stock OR water plus stock cube
seasoned flour	
1 oz. butter	4 oz. long grain rice
3 onions, sliced	½ level teaspoon salt

First meal

1 Ask the butcher to bone and roll the meat. Roll in seasoned flour and then brown in the hot butter in a large saucepan.

2 Lift the meat from the pan and add the onion and carrot; sauté gently for 5–10 minutes to soften. Then replace the meat, add the stock and cover with a lid.

3 Simmer gently for 1¼ hours. When tender lift the meat from the pan and strain the stock. Place the meat and vegetables on a hot serving platter to keep warm.

4 Measure ½ pint of the cooking broth into a saucepan, add the rice and salt. Bring to the boil, stir once and then cover with a lid and cook very gently for 20 minutes, or until the rice is tender and the liquid absorbed.

5 Serve the meat sliced, with braised vegetables and cooked rice.

Second meal

for the stovies:

leftover cooked lamb	2 onions, sliced
½ oz. dripping	¼ pint stock OR water plus stock cube
2 potatoes, sliced	

For the stovies, slice the cold cooked lamb fairly thinly and cut into small pieces. Heat enough dripping to cover the base of a saucepan, then add layers of potato slices, sliced onion and meat scraps. Add ¼ pint of stock or water plus a cube, season well and cover with a lid. Set over a very low heat and cook gently for 1–1½ hours, or until the potatoes are tender.

Braised half shoulder of lamb and Shepherd's pie

you will need:

½ shoulder of lamb	2 stalks celery, scrubbed and sliced
salt and pepper	
1 oz. dripping	1 level tablespoon flour
1 rasher streaky bacon	½ pint stock OR water plus stock cube
2 small onions, sliced	

First meal

1 Wipe the shoulder of lamb and season.

2 Heat the dripping in a saucepan, add the trimmed and chopped bacon rasher and prepared vegetables. Cook gently over moderate heat to soften a little and brown lightly.

3 Lift the vegetables out, put in a 2-pint oven-proof casserole dish and place joint on top.

continued

4 Add the flour to the hot fat in the pan and fry gently until frothy and beginning to brown. Stir in the hot stock and bring to the boil.

5 Season if necessary then strain over the contents of the casserole dish.

6 Cover, place in the centre of a slow oven (335°F. – Gas Mark 3) and braise for 2½–3 hours. Serve with the cooked vegetables and strained gravy.

Second meal

for the pie:	pinch mixed herbs
leftover cooked meat	⅓ pint stock and 1 table-
1 onion, finely sliced	spoon flour (if no
½ oz. butter	gravy)
salt and pepper	3 medium potatoes,
¼ level teaspoon curry	cooked
powder	

For the shepherd's pie, mince the meat scraps. Fry onion gently in butter until soft. Add the meat, salt and pepper, curry powder, pinch of mixed herbs. Moisten with gravy left over from the joint, or stock thickened with 1 tablespoon flour. Heat the mixture through and spoon into a buttered 1–1½-pint pie dish. Top with mashed potato and place in the centre of a moderate oven (355°F. – Gas Mark 4). Heat through for 30 minutes.

Roast chicken with oatmeal stuffing and Chicken vol-au-vent

you will need:

small (2–2½ lb.) oven-ready roasting chicken	for the stuffing:
	6 oz. medium oatmeal
½ lemon	3 oz. shredded beef
salt and pepper	suet
2 oz. butter OR dripping	1 large onion, finely
few rashers streaky bacon	chopped
flour	salt and pepper

First meal

1 If using a frozen bird, allow 6–8 hours to thaw out. Rinse the bird and pat dry with a clean cloth. Rub the inside of the bird with a little salt and the outside with a cut lemon.

2 Measure the oatmeal into a basin, add the suet, onion and seasoning and mix well.

3 Stuff the neck cavity of the bird with a little of the stuffing. Pull the neck skin over the stuffing underneath the bird, twisting the wing tips forward and under and secure with a skewer.

4 Place the prepared chicken in a roasting tin. Smear the body of the chicken with a little of the butter or dripping and place the remainder in the tin. (If you prefer to cook the chicken unstuffed, place another 2-oz. lump of butter inside the bird to keep it moist.)

5 Cover the breast with the trimmed bacon rashers and a piece of kitchen foil.

6 Place in the centre of a moderately hot oven (380°F. – Gas Mark 5) and roast, allowing 20 minutes per lb. plus 20 minutes, basting frequently.

7 About ¼ hour before cooking is completed, remove the foil and bacon rashers, dredge the breast with a little flour and return to oven to brown.

8 Prepare gravy made as page 18, but using stock made from giblets. Serve with bread sauce, roast potatoes and cauliflower.

Second meal

for the vol-au-vent:	⅓ pint milk
leftover chicken flesh	2 oz. mushrooms,
1 oz. butter	sliced
1 tablespoon flour	4 vol-au-vent cases

For chicken vol-au-vent, remove all the cooked chicken flesh from the carcass and shred into suitably sized pieces. In a saucepan melt 1 oz. butter and stir in 1 tablespoon flour. Cook gently over low heat for 1 minute, then gradually add ⅓ pint milk to make a smooth sauce. Season and add the chicken flesh and 2 oz. sliced mushrooms sautéed in a little butter for 2–3 minutes. Spoon into hot vol-au-vent cases (buy these ready-made, or prepare your own from a small packet frozen puff pastry). Serve hot with green peas.

Roast pigeons

you will need:

2 pigeons	2 streaky bacon
1½ oz. butter	rashers
2 small bay leaves	flour

1 Season pigeons and place ½ oz. butter and a bay leaf inside each one.

2 Smear breasts with remaining butter, cover with trimmed and halved bacon rashers and place in a small roasting or baking tin.

3 Cover with buttered paper, place in the centre of a moderately hot oven (375°F. – Gas Mark 5) and roast for 1 hour.

4 Remove the buttered paper and bacon rashers, dredge the breasts with a little flour, baste and replace high up in the oven to brown – takes about 10 minutes.

5 Serve with gravy, bread sauce, sauté potatoes and braised celery.

Beef pot roast and Beef with savoury brown gravy

you will need:

1 small piece topside of beef (1–1½ lb.)	½ pint stock OR water plus stock cube
salt and pepper	1 level teaspoon corn-
1 oz. lard OR dripping	flour
1 onion, sliced	cold water to blend
4 carrots, sliced	

First meal

1 Wipe the meat and check that it is firmly tied with string or skewered. Season.
2 In a saucepan melt the lard or dripping and add the meat, brown well on both sides over fairly high heat.
3 Lower the heat, add the prepared vegetables, sprinkle with salt and pepper and pour in the stock. Cover with tight-fitting lid and simmer very gently for 1½–2 hours or until the meat is tender, adding little extra boiling stock if necessary.
4 Lift the meat from the pan and place with the vegetables on a hot serving platter. Allow to stand 5 minutes while preparing the gravy.
5 Blend the cornflour with cold water to make a smooth paste, then stir into the gravy and bring to the boil, stirring all the time. Check seasoning and strain gravy into a gravy boat. Serve the meat sliced, with gravy, vegetables and roast potatoes.

Second meal

for beef with gravy:	cold water to blend
leftover sliced meat	½ pint stock OR water
2 rounded teaspoons flour	and stock cube
1 rounded teaspoon gravy thickening powder	

Serve any leftover meat sliced and heated through in the following *savoury brown gravy*: in a small mixing basin blend flour and gravy thickening powder with cold water to make a smooth paste. Gradually stir in hot stock, strain into a pan and re-heat stirring until boiling and thickened.

Baked spiced gammon and Bacon fritters

you will need:

1 piece of gammon slipper (about 2 lb.)	Demerara sugar
little French mustard	few cloves

First meal

1 Make sure how much your joint weighs so you can calculate cooking time. Soak in cold water for several hours or overnight. Drain, place in a saucepan skin side down and cover with fresh cold water.
2 Bring slowly to the boil and remove any scum that rises. As soon as it reaches boiling point, lower the heat and simmer, covered, for 20 minutes to each lb. and 20 minutes extra. Top the pan up with extra boiling water if necessary to keep the joint covered.
3 Lift the cooked joint from the hot liquor and strip off the rind. Place in a roasting tin, and spread the fat with a little mustard and coat with sugar. Using a small sharp knife, score the fat in a criss-cross design and stud with the cloves.
4 Crisp off in the centre of a moderate oven (355°F. – Gas Mark 4) for about 10 minutes. Serve with apple sauce, parsley, roast potatoes and buttered broccoli spears.

Second meal

for the fritters:	toasted breadcrumbs
leftover bacon	to coat
1 egg	lard OR dripping

For the bacon fritters, dip the cold bacon slices, fairly thickly cut, first in a little beaten egg, then in breadcrumbs and fry in hot lard or dripping until golden brown. Serve with grilled tomatoes and chipped potatoes.

Breast of lamb with sausage stuffing, hot or cold

you will need:

1 breast of lamb, boned	½ small onion, finely chopped
	1 level teaspoon dry
for the stuffing:	mustard
4 oz. pork sausage meat	1 level teaspoon salt
4 oz. fresh white breadcrumbs	pinch pepper
	3 tablespoons milk OR stock
1 rounded tablespoon chopped parsley	1 oz. lard OR dripping

First meal

1 Trim the breast of lamb and lay the meat flat, skin side downwards. Set aside while preparing the stuffing.
2 Mix together the sausage meat, breadcrumbs, parsley, onion, seasoning and enough milk or stock to make a moist consistency.
3 Spread the lamb evenly with the stuffing and roll up from one end. Tie in several places with string or secure with skewers.
4 Stand in a roasting tin, smear the joint with a little of the fat or dripping and place rest of fat in the tin.
5 Place in the centre of a moderate oven (355°F. – Gas Mark 4) and roast, basting occasionally, for 1¼ hours. *continued*

6 Transfer to a hot platter and slice thinly. Serve with sauté or roast potatoes and a green vegetable.

Second meal

Serve remaining sliced lamb cold, with potato salad, tomatoes tossed in oil and vinegar dressing, and crisp lettuce.

Pork sausage galantine, hot and cold

you will need:

4 oz. bacon rashers	1 teaspoon Worcester-
1 onion, finely chopped	shire sauce
1 lb. pork sausage meat	1 level teaspoon dry
1 oz. fresh white bread-	mustard
crumbs	salt and pepper
1 level tablespoon	1 egg
chopped parsley	1–2 tablespoons stock
pinch mixed herbs	OR water
1 tablespoon chutney	

First meal

1 Snip away the rind and chop the bacon finely. Sauté gently with the onions until quite soft (about 5 minutes).
2 Then add to the sausage meat, with the breadcrumbs, parsley, mixed herbs, chutney (with large pieces chopped), Worcestershire sauce, mustard and seasoning.
3 Add the egg and enough stock or water to mix to a fairly soft consistency.
4 Pack the mixture into a lightly greased 1½-pint pudding basin, cover with double layers of greased greaseproof or kitchen foil and steam gently for 1½–2 hours.
5 Cover remainder with fresh paper, top with a saucer and a heavy weight and leave overnight until quite cold.

Second meal

Any leftover meat may be served thinly sliced with potato salad, sliced tomatoes, cucumber marinaded in French dressing and tossed lettuce.

Roast half-leg of lamb and Lamb and potato cakes

you will need:

1 small half-leg of lamb	**for the gravy:**
salt and pepper	1 tablespoon flour
flour	½ pint stock OR
1–2 oz. dripping OR	vegetable water
lard	salt and pepper

First meal

1 Wipe the meat and weigh to calculate the cooking time. Season, dredge with a little flour and rub well in, particularly over fatty parts, for a crisp golden finish.

2 Place the meat in a small roasting pan, smear with a little of the dripping and place the remainder in the pan.
3 Place in the centre of a hot oven (425°F. – Gas Mark 7) and when fat begins to spit, reduce heat to moderate (355°F. – Gas Mark 4) for the rest of cooking time.
4 Allow 25 minutes per lb. plus 25 minutes, and baste occasionally (for a joint less than 3 lb. reduce cooking time by 5 minutes per lb.)
5 About 20 minutes before cooking time is completed, turn the joint and baste again. Lift from pan on to a hot platter and allow to stand for 5 minutes while preparing the gravy.
6 Pour away all but 1 tablespoon of the dripping, stir flour into this, cook until frothy, then stir in hot stock. Season and bring to the boil. Cook for 2–3 minutes, then strain into a hot gravy boat and serve with the meat.

Second meal

for the cakes:	1 egg
leftover lamb	toasted breadcrumbs
cooked potato	to coat
salt and pepper	lard OR dripping
Worcestershire sauce	

For the lamb and potato cakes, in a basin combine together equal quantities of minced or finely chopped leftover meat and cooked mashed potatoes. Season well, add a dash of Worcestershire sauce, and just enough lightly beaten egg to bind the mixture. Divide into approximately four portions and shape into patties. Dip first in remaining beaten egg and then in toasted breadcrumbs. Pat coating firmly and fry in hot lard or dripping until golden brown on both sides, and heated through (about 10 minutes). Serve with green peas and grilled tomatoes.

Old-fashioned meat roll and Meat roll fritters

you will need:

10 oz. rump steak OR	½ level teaspoon salt
lean stewing steak	pinch pepper
4 oz. lean bacon	1 small egg
1 teacup fresh white	brown breadcrumbs
breadcrumbs	for coating

First meal

1 Grease a stone 1-lb. jar and a paper to cover (a stone marmalade jar will do).
2 Mince the meat and bacon twice. Add the white breadcrumbs, salt and pepper and beaten egg.
3 Mix well together until evenly blended and moist. Then pack into greased jar and cover with the paper tied firmly with string.
4 Steam gently for 2–2½ hours.
5 Cover with fresh paper, set a weight on top, and

leave overnight. Approximately 15 minutes before serving, carefully remove the meat roll from the jar, warming base gently if necessary. Coat with browned breadcrumbs and slice. Serve with buttered potatoes or potato salad and tossed lettuce.

Second meal

for the fritters:

leftover meat roll	toasted breadcrumbs
1 egg	to coat

Slice remaining meat roll and dip slices first in beaten egg and then in toasted breadcrumbs. Pat coating on firmly and fry in hot fat until golden brown on either side. Serve with chipped potatoes and fried mushrooms.

Hot semolina with sultanas

you will need:

½ pint milk	1 rounded tablespoon
1 level tablespoon	castor sugar
semolina	1 oz. sultanas

1 Heat the milk gently in a saucepan rinsed out with cold water (to prevent sticking) and when hot sprinkle in the semolina, stirring all the time.
2 Bring to the boil and add the sugar, lower the heat and cook gently for about 5 minutes, stirring occasionally.
3 Draw the pan off the heat and add the sultanas. Pour the mixture into a buttered 1-pint baking or pie dish.
4 Place in the centre of a slow oven (335°F. – Gas Mark 3) and bake for 30 minutes. Serve with cream or top of the milk.

Rice pudding

you will need:

1 level tablespoon	½ pint milk
round grain OR	½ oz. butter
pudding rice	1 tablespoon evapor-
1 level tablespoon	ated milk OR cream
castor sugar	

1 Well butter a ½-pint baking dish and over the base sprinkle in the rice and sugar.
2 Pour in the milk, stir to mix and dot the surface with pieces of butter.
3 Place in the centre of a slow oven (310°F. – Gas Mark 2) and bake for two hours.
4 To get a really smooth creamy rice pudding, stir in the first three skins as they form during the first ½ hour of cooking. After stirring in the third skin, add the evaporated milk or cream and leave to brown.
5 Serve with top of the milk or cream.

Eve's pudding and Cake custards

you will need:

	for the cake topping:
1 medium-sized	2 oz. butter OR
cooking apple,	margarine
pared and sliced	2 oz. castor sugar
1 tablespoon water	1 egg
1 tablespoon castor	few drops vanilla
sugar	essence
	3 oz. self-raising flour
	little milk to mix

First meal

1 Prepare the fruit and place in the centre of a greased 1-pint pie dish, with the water and sugar. Set aside and prepare the topping.
2 Cream together the butter and sugar until light, then gradually beat in the lightly mixed egg and essence. Fold in the sieved flour, and just enough milk to mix to a soft consistency.
3 Spoon the cake mixture over the apple in the pie dish, and spread evenly.
4 Place in the centre of a moderate oven (355°F. – Gas Mark 4) and bake for 35 minutes or until risen and brown.

Second meal

for cake custards:

leftover pudding	¼ pint milk
1 tablespoon custard	castor sugar to taste
powder	walnuts

Spoon leftover pudding into 2 individual glass serving dishes. In a small basin blend 1 tablespoon custard powder with a little of the cold milk to a thin paste. Stir in remaining milk and strain into a saucepan.
Stir over moderate heat until boiling and thickened. Draw the pan off the heat, sweeten custard to taste with castor sugar and, when slightly cool, pour over the pudding. Sprinkle with chopped walnuts and chill until ready to serve. Serve with top of the milk.

Caramel custards, hot and cold

you will need:

	for the custard:
2 oz. granulated sugar	3 eggs
1 tablespoon water	milk
	2 oz. castor sugar

1 Heat the granulated sugar in a heavy saucepan over moderate heat until melted and golden brown.
2 Draw the pan off the heat and add the water – *take care at this stage as the mixture will boil furiously.* Return to the heat and stir until caramel has melted and dissolved. *continued*

3 Pour a little of the caramel into the base of each of four small ¼-pint baking dishes or moulds. Set aside while preparing the custard.

4 Crack the eggs into a measuring jug, and make up to 1 pint with milk. Whisk eggs, milk and sugar together lightly, then strain the mixture into the caramel-lined moulds – filling each one to the top.

5 Place the moulds in a shallow roasting tin, with 1 inch cold water, set on a low shelf of a slow oven (310°F. – Gas Mark 2) and bake for 1 hour until the custards have set.

6 Allow to cool for 5 minutes, then turn out and serve 2 of the moulds with cream off the top of the milk. The remaining 2 can be kept in the moulds in a cool place to serve cold the next day.

Skilful cooking on a budget

There are times when we all have to be careful – and for some of us it's all the time. Remember that thrifty housekeeping takes time, effort and careful planning. Regard it as a challenge to your skill as a cook and it will cease to be a bore. Plan your meals ahead and work out a detailed shopping list. Menus made up when you reach the shops always cost more. Watch prices and choose foods that will give you good quality at a low price. Buy cheaper cuts of meat for braising and stewing and make full use of a pressure cooker if you have one. Take care when selecting tinned foods; some are better quality than others so read the labels carefully and get to know the brands you like best.

Never throw away scraps of leftover food – see pages 56 to 62 for ideas on using up and collect as many recipes as you can find.

Eggs in onion sauce

you will need:

3 eggs

for the sauce:	
1 oz. butter OR margarine	salt and pepper
	pinch cayenne
1 onion, finely chopped	4 oz. long grain rice
1 level teaspoon flour	
½ pint milk	**to garnish:**
	chopped parsley

1 Hard-boil the eggs, plunge into cold water, peel then cut in halves lengthwise. Set aside while preparing the sauce.

2 Melt the butter or margarine in a saucepan over low heat, add the onion and sauté gently until soft (about 5 minutes). Stir in the flour and cook for 1 minute. Gradually stir in the milk, beating well all the time to get a really smooth sauce.

3 Bring to the boil, season with salt and pepper and cayenne, add the eggs and simmer for 2–3 minutes.

4 Sprinkle the rice into a pan of boiling salted water, and cook briskly for 10 minutes until tender. Drain and return to the hot pan to steam dry for a few minutes.

5 Spoon the hot rice on to a serving dish and spoon the egg and onion sauce over the rice. Sprinkle with chopped parsley and serve.

Tomato rice casserole

you will need:

2 oz. long grain rice	6 oz. grated Cheddar cheese
1 can condensed cream of tomato soup	1 egg, slightly beaten
1 soup can water	½ oz. butter
¼ level teaspoon salt	1 heaped tablespoon fresh white bread-crumbs
pinch of cayenne pepper	

1 Wash the rice in cold water, drain and place in a saucepan. Stir in the condensed tomato soup and the water.

2 Add the seasoning, cover with a lid and bring up to the boil. Lower the heat, cover with a lid and simmer gently for 30–35 minutes until the rice is tender. Stir occasionally to prevent burning.

3 Draw the pan off the heat and stir in 4 oz. of the cheese and the egg.

4 Pour into a buttered 1–1½ pint baking dish.

5 Melt the butter in a small saucepan. Draw the pan off the heat and using a fork, stir in the breadcrumbs and remaining cheese. When the butter is absorbed, sprinkle over the top of the casserole.

6 Place above centre in a hot oven (400°F. – Gas Mark 6) and bake for 10–15 minutes or until brown and crisp.

Serve at once with slices of buttered toast.

Egg and onion casserole

you will need:

3 eggs	¼ pint milk
2 onions	salt and pepper
1½ oz. butter OR margarine	2 oz. grated Cheddar cheese
1 level tablespoon flour	

1 Hard-boil the eggs, remove the shells, and slice in half.

2 Peel and slice the onions, and fry gently in 1 oz. of the butter or margarine until soft and golden brown (about 10 minutes).

3 Meanwhile melt the remaining margarine in a saucepan and stir in the flour. Gradually beat in the milk, beating well to get a really smooth sauce.

4 Season and simmer for 2–3 minutes.

5 Spoon the cooked onions over the base of the casserole dish and arrange the egg halves round sides and over the top. Pour over the sauce, sprinkle with the cheese and grill until golden brown and bubbling hot.

6 Serve with creamed potatoes.

Potato cheese

you will need:

1 lb. potatoes	1 level tablespoon flour
1 onion, peeled and chopped	⅓ pint (or 1 teacupful) milk
salt and pepper	4 oz. grated Cheddar
½ oz. butter	cheese

1 Peel and slice the potatoes about ¼ inch thick. Plunge into boiling water and cook for 4–5 minutes then drain.

2 Arrange alternate layers of potato and chopped onion in a buttered 1½-pint pie dish. Season each layer with salt and pepper.

3 Melt the butter in a saucepan and stir in the flour. Cook gently for 1 minute. Gradually stir in the milk beating well all the time to get a really smooth sauce.

4 Bring up to the boil, season with salt and pepper and simmer gently for 2–3 minutes.

5 Stir in half the cheese and then pour the sauce over the potatoes. Cover with a well-buttered paper and a lid, place in the centre of a slow oven (310°F. – Gas Mark 2) and cook for about 2 hours.

6 When cooked remove the paper and the lid, top with remaining grated cheese and grill until brown. Serve with grilled sausages.

Cheese eggs

you will need:

	for the sauce:
1 lb. potatoes	½ oz. butter
salt and pepper	1 level tablespoon flour
½ oz. butter	⅓ pint milk
little milk	seasoning
2 hard-boiled eggs	2 oz. grated cheese

1 Peel and boil the potatoes. When cooked, mash with plenty of seasoning and the butter. Add a little milk and beat well until smooth and creamy.

2 Spoon the mashed potato into a buttered 1½-pint baking or pie dish, spread over the sides and across the base to make a nest shape. Keep warm.

3 Prepare the sauce. Melt the butter in a small pan and stir in the flour. Cook over low heat for 1 minute. Gradually add milk and bring to boil, stirring well all the time to get a smooth sauce.

4 Season to taste, add half the cheese and cook over low heat 2–3 minutes.

5 Draw the pan off the heat, add the sliced hard-boiled eggs and pour into the centre of the potato nest. Top with remaining cheese and grill until bubbling hot and golden brown.

6 Serve immediately with buttered broccoli spears or grilled tomatoes.

Cheese fillets

you will need:

½ pint milk	3 oz. finely grated Cheddar cheese
½ onion, stuck with a clove	
1 small bay leaf	**for the coating:**
2 oz. fine semolina	1 egg
1 tablespoon chopped parsley	toasted breadcrumbs
salt and pepper	corn oil for deep frying
¼ level teaspoon dry mustard	

1 Measure the milk, onion and bay leaf into a saucepan. Place over moderate heat and bring almost up to the boil, then draw the pan off the heat and leave to infuse for 15 minutes.

2 Strain the milk and return to the pan, reboil and sprinkle in the semolina. Cook until very thick stirring all the time – takes about 6 minutes.

3 Draw the pan off the heat and beat in the parsley, a good seasoning of salt and pepper, the mustard and cheese.

4 Spread the mixture evenly over a small wet plate and leave until quite cold. Mixture should be about ½ inch thick.

5 Cut into four sections and coat each first in lightly beaten egg and then in toasted breadcrumbs. Fry in the hot deep fat for 2–3 minutes, until golden brown on both sides.

6 Drain and serve with a tossed salad or grilled tomatoes.

Braised lamb's tongues

you will need:

	for the sauce:
3 lamb's tongues	½ pint cooking liquor
8 oz. carrots, sliced	½ oz. butter OR margarine
2 large onions, sliced	
1 pint water OR stock	2 rounded teaspoons flour
	salt and pepper

1 Rinse the tongues and place them in a deep stewpan, on top of prepared vegetables.

2 Add the water or stock, then cover with a tight-fitting lid and bring to the boil. Lower the heat and allow to simmer gently for 1½–2 hours. Alternatively, cook in pressure cooker at 15 lb. pressure for 30 minutes.

3 Reserve cooking liquor. Allow cooked tongues to cool 5 minutes then remove the skin and core

continued

at the base. Skin the tongues, slice in half and place in a casserole, adding the carrots and a little onion.

4 For the sauce, bring ½ pint cooking liquor to the boil.

5 Melt the butter or margarine, add flour and allow to cook until the mixture is a dark nutty brown.

6 Gradually stir in the boiling liquor; reboil the sauce, stirring well until thickened, then season and simmer for 5 minutes.

7 Pour over the tongues and heat thoroughly. Serve with Brussels sprouts and creamed potatoes.

Baked fish cutlets

you will need:

2 tail-end cod cutlets
salt and pepper

for the stuffing:	little finely grated
1 rounded tablespoon fresh white bread-crumbs	lemon rind
	¼ oz. butter OR margarine
1 teaspoon finely chopped parsley	
pinch mixed herbs	to garnish:
	lemon slices
	melted butter

1 Rinse the fish cutlets and trim away the fins with scissors. Snip out the centre bone, then season the cutlets and place in a well-buttered baking dish. Set aside and prepare the stuffing.

2 In a small basin combine the breadcrumbs, parsley, mixed herbs and grated lemon rind. Melt the butter and mix into the ingredients with a fork – the stuffing should be moist and crumbly.

3 Pack the stuffing into the centre of the fish cutlets.

4 Cover with a well-buttered paper and lid. Place in the centre of a moderate oven (335°F. – Gas Mark 4) and bake for 20–25 minutes.

5 Serve the cutlets immediately topped with lemon slices and with extra melted butter, sauté potatoes and French beans.

Rice croquettes

you will need:

4 oz. long grain rice	¼ level teaspoon made mustard
1 oz. butter or margarine	4 oz. grated cheese
1 level tablespoon flour	1 egg, lightly beaten
¼ pint (or 1 teacupful) milk	toasted breadcrumbs
salt and pepper	corn oil for deep frying

1 Add the rice to plenty of boiling water and cook briskly for 10 minutes. Drain and set aside.

2 Melt the fat in a saucepan over low heat and stir in the flour. Cook gently for 1 minute.

3 Gradually stir in the milk, beating well all the time to get a really smooth sauce. Bring to the boil and season well. Cook gently for 2–3 minutes.

4 Stir in the mustard and cheese and when blended draw the pan off the heat and stir in the cooked rice.

5 Pour the mixture out into a buttered shallow baking tin or plate, and leave until quite cold. Mixture should be at least ½ inch thick.

6 Cut the mixture into four portions and shape each one into a croquette. Dip first into the beaten egg and then in the toasted breadcrumbs. Fry in the hot oil until golden brown and crisp. Drain and serve with grilled mushrooms or buttered French beans.

Mushroom risotto

you will need:

6 oz. long grain rice	¾ pint stock OR water plus stock cube
4 lean bacon rashers	
½ onion, chopped	4 oz. mushrooms
2 oz. butter OR margarine	3 oz. grated cheese

1 Wash the rice, trim the bacon rashers and chop up two of them. Sauté both gently for 5 minutes with onion in 1 oz. of the butter. Stir to prevent browning.

2 Gradually add the hot stock and bring to the boil. Lower the heat, cover with a lid and simmer very gently for 20–30 minutes until the liquid is absorbed and the rice quite tender.

3 Trim and slice the mushrooms and sauté gently for 2–3 minutes in remaining butter.

4 When the rice is cooked add the mushrooms with half the grated cheese and blend in with a fork.

5 Turn the risotto into a hot serving dish and sprinkle with remaining cheese. Garnish with reserved bacon rashers halved, rolled and grilled on a skewer.

6 Serve with crusty French bread and butter or tossed green salad.

Variation

Chicken liver risotto – follow the recipe above, omitting the cheese and adding 3–4 oz. chicken livers, trimmed and sliced, together with the rice, chopped bacon rashers and onion in first stage of recipe.

Hamburgers

you will need:

8 oz. minced beef	1 heaped tablespoon
½ level teaspoon salt	fresh white bread-
¼ level teaspoon	crumbs
pepper	little mixed egg
pinch of sage OR	1 oz. lard OR dripping
thyme	for frying
¼ small onion, finely	
grated or minced	

1 Put the mince, salt and pepper and herbs in a basin. Add the onion, breadcrumbs and enough egg to bind the mixture together.
2 Mix the ingredients with a fork. Take care to mix to a soft *but not sticky* consistency – the mixture should cling together when pressed lightly into shape.
3 Divide into 4 equal portions and shape each into a patty about 3 inches wide. Flatten lightly with a spatula or knife blade.
4 To fry the hamburgers, cook gently over medium heat in hot fat. Allow to cook for 5–6 minutes, turning them once. If you prefer to grill the hamburgers, put under a hot grill about 3 inches from the heat. Allow 8–12 minutes, turning them once.
5 Serve with chipped potatoes and green peas or baked beans; or sandwich in a toasted soft roll, topped with mustard and onion rings.

Variations

Hamburger mixed grill – serve hamburgers with tomato halves, season and grill 10 minutes; peel mushroom caps, season and grill for 5–8 minutes.
With bacon and banana – or grill trimmed bacon rashers 2 minutes, and grill banana halves 4 minutes each side.
Serve with a tossed green salad.

Cheese tartlets

you will need:

3 oz. plain flour	**for the filling:**
1½ oz. butter or	1 egg
margarine	2 tablespoons milk
water to mix	2 oz. grated Cheddar
	cheese

1 Sift the flour and salt into a mixing basin, rub in the fat and stir in sufficient water to mix a firm dough. Turn out on to a floured working surface and knead lightly.
2 Roll out thinly and using a 2–2½-inch round cutter, stamp out about 8 circles of pastry and use these to line 8 greased tartlet tins.
3 In a mixing basin combine together the egg, milk and cheese, and mix well and spoon into the unbaked tartlet cases.
4 Place on a baking tray, and set above the centre

in a hot oven (400°F. – Gas Mark 6) and bake for 10 minutes. Then lower the heat to fairly hot (380°F. – Gas Mark 5) and bake for a further 5 minutes.
5 Serve hot with grilled tomatoes or mushrooms.

Cheese soufflé

you will need:

1 oz. butter OR	3 oz. Cheddar cheese
margarine	½ teaspoon made
1 oz. plain flour	mustard
¼ pint milk	3 eggs
salt and pepper	

1 Lightly butter a 5–6-inch round soufflé or baking dish and set aside.
2 Melt the butter in a saucepan and stir in the flour. Cook gently for 1 minute but do not brown.
3 Gradually stir in the milk, beating well all the time to get a really smooth sauce. Bring to the boil, lower the heat and cook gently for 2–3 minutes.
4 Season to taste, add the grated cheese and mustard and stir until smooth and blended.
5 Draw the pan off the heat. Allow to cool, and beat in the egg yolks.
6 In a basin whisk the egg whites until stiff, then fold into the cheese mixture with a metal spoon.
7 Pour into the prepared dish, place in the centre of a moderate oven (355°F. – Gas Mark 4) and bake for 25–30 minutes or until risen and browned.
8 Serve at once with grilled tomatoes or sautéed mushrooms.

Variations

Onion soufflé – proceed as for the basic cheese recipe but omit two tablespoons of milk and the mustard and cheese. Instead put 8 oz. onions in a saucepan. Cover with cold salted water and bring to the boil. Simmer gently for 25–30 minutes until tender, then drain and mince finely.
Stir the onion into the hot and thickened sauce mixture and season with 1 level teaspoon salt, ¼ level teaspoon onion salt, and a good pinch of pepper. Add a little crushed garlic, if liked.
Cool the sauce as in the basic recipe, then beat in the egg yolks and fold in the beaten egg whites. Pour the mixture into a buttered 6–7-inch soufflé dish and bake in the centre of a moderate oven (355°F. – Gas Mark 4) for 35–40 minutes.
Smoked fish soufflé – proceed as for cheese recipe, but omit the mustard and cheese. Instead place 8 oz. smoked cod fillet in a saucepan and cover with ¼ pint milk, taken from the milk in the basic recipe – this way you add extra flavour to the sauce. *continued*

Bring the milk to the boil, cover the pan with a lid and simmer gently for 10–15 minutes or until the fish is tender. Draw the pan off the heat, drain and reserve the milk, making it up to the required quantity with fresh milk.

Flake the fish, discarding any bones or skin. Add the flaked fish to the prepared basic sauce, season with ½ level teaspoon salt, good pinch of pepper and 1 level teaspoon curry powder. Cool slightly as in the basic recipe, then beat in the egg yolks and fold in the beaten whites.

Pour the mixture into a buttered 6–7-inch soufflé dish and bake in the centre of a moderate oven (355°F. – Gas Mark 4) for 35–40 minutes. Serve immediately.

Cheese and potato patties

you will need:

1 lb. potatoes	1 tablespoon chopped
salt and pepper	parsley
1 egg	toasted breadcrumbs
4 oz. grated Cheddar	for coating
cheese	3–4 tablespoons
¼ teaspoon made	ground nut oil for
mustard	frying

1 Peel, boil and mash the potato with plenty of seasoning.
2 Beat the egg lightly and add just enough to the potato to bind the mixture together.
3 Stir in the grated cheese, mustard and parsley. Turn the mixture out on to a lightly floured working surface, and divide into 4 portions.
4 Shape each portion into a round patty, and then dip first in the beaten egg and then in the toasted breadcrumbs.
5 Put in the hot oil over moderate heat and fry until golden brown on both sides. Drain and serve hot with fried eggs.

Macaroni cheese and tomato

you will need:

2–3 oz. quick-cooking	1 level tablespoon flour
macaroni	¼ pint milk
3 tomatoes	salt and pepper
	¼ level teaspoon made
for the cheese sauce:	mustard
1 oz. butter OR	2–3 oz. grated Cheddar
margarine	cheese

1 Add macaroni to plenty of boiling salted water and allow to cook for 7 minutes. When cooked drain and rinse for 1 minute under hot water.
2 Plunge the tomatoes into boiling water for 1 minute and peel off the skins. Slice one and set aside for the top, deseed and coarsely chop the

remainder. Set aside while preparing the cheese sauce.
3 Melt the butter or margarine in a saucepan over moderate heat. Stir in the flour and cook gently 1 minute, but do not allow to brown.
4 Gradually stir in the milk, beating well all the time to get a smooth sauce. Bring to the boil, season well, add the mustard and half the grated cheese.
5 Cook gently for 5 minutes then draw the pan off the heat and add the cooked macaroni and chopped tomato flesh.
6 Pour into a hot buttered serving dish. Top with rows of tomato slices and the remaining grated cheese.
7 Grill until bubbling hot then serve at once with hot buttered toast.

Sweet corn omelet

you will need:

4 eggs	1 7-oz. tin creamed
1 tablespoon water	style sweet corn
salt and pepper	butter
¼ level teaspoon curry	
powder	

1 Whisk together the eggs, water and seasoning of salt and pepper and the curry powder.
2 Stir in the sweet corn.
3 Heat the butter in an 8 inch omelet or frying pan and when bubbling hot pour in all the omelet mixture at once.
4 Using a fork, stir over moderate heat until beginning to set. Then leave until browned on the underside.
5 Loosen edges and fold opposites into centre. Push the omelet to one side of the pan and turn out on to a hot plate. Slice in half and serve at once with a tossed salad.

Canneloni with spinach and cheese sauce

you will need:

6 canneloni shells	1 level tablespoon flour
1 small packet chopped	¼ pint (or 1 teacupful)
spinach	milk
	salt and pepper
for the cheese sauce:	3 oz. grated Cheddar
1 oz. butter OR	cheese
margarine	

1 Add the canneloni shells to a pan of boiling, salted water and boil briskly for 15–20 minutes.
2 Meanwhile heat the spinach according to packet directions and season with salt and pepper.
3 Drain the cooked canneloni and stuff each one with spinach. Arrange in a buttered baking or

pie dish and set aside while preparing the sauce.

4 Melt the fat in a saucepan and stir in the flour. Cook for 1 minute.

5 Gradually beat in the milk stirring well all the time to get a smooth sauce. Bring up to the boil, season well and cook for 2–3 minutes, then stir in half the cheese.

6 Pour the hot sauce over the canneloni, sprinkle with reserved cheese and place above centre in a moderately hot oven (380°F. – Gas Mark 5). Bake for 20 minutes or until bubbling hot and browned. Serve with a tossed salad.

Minced beef and onion

you will need:

½ oz. lard OR dripping	½ pint stock OR water
1 onion, finely chopped	plus stock cube
8 oz. minced beef	salt and pepper
1 level tablespoon flour	little gravy browning

1 Heat the dripping or lard and gently fry the onion until soft. Add the minced beef and fry, stirring occasionally, until browned.

2 Stir in the flour and then the stock, seasoning and a few drops of gravy browning.

3 Bring to the boil and simmer gently for 30 minutes.

4 Serve with creamed potatoes garnished with chopped parsley or snipped chives, and boiled cabbage.

Marinated cod cutlets

you will need:

2 tail-end cod cutlets	½ onion, finely chopped
	¼ level teaspoon salt
for the marinade:	pinch pepper
3 tablespoons salad oil	
1½ tablespoons	flour OR fresh white
vinegar	breadcrumbs to coat
juice ¼ lemon	2 oz. butter for frying
1 tablespoon chopped	
parsley	

1 Trim the cod cutlets, place in a shallow dish.

2 To prepare the marinade, combine together the oil, vinegar, lemon juice, parsley, onion and seasoning. Mix well then pour over the cod cutlets and leave to marinate for 1 hour, turning occasionally.

3 Lift from the marinade, allowing excess to drain away, then coat in flour or fresh white breadcrumbs.

4 Fry in hot fat over moderate heat, turning to brown evenly. Fry for 8–10 minutes until golden brown on both sides.

5 Serve with grilled tomatoes, chipped potatoes and baked beans.

Sausage supper

you will need:

8 oz. pork or beef	¼ teaspoon Worcester-
chipolata sausages	shire sauce
1 onion, sliced	pinch mixed herbs
1 green pepper, seeded	¼ level teaspoon sugar
and sliced	pepper and salt
1 8-oz. tin tomatoes	

1 Place the sausages in a cold frying pan, set over moderate heat and cook gently until browned. Lift out into a casserole dish.

2 Add the onion to the fat in the pan and fry gently until soft (about 5 minutes). Then add the green pepper and fry for a few minutes more.

3 Stir in the tomatoes plus liquid from the tin, Worcestershire sauce, herbs, sugar and seasoning. Bring to the boil, then pour over the sausages.

4 Cover the casserole with a lid and place in the centre of a moderately hot oven (380°F. – Gas Mark 5) and cook 20–30 minutes.

5 Serve sausages with the contents of the casserole spooned over the top, accompanied by creamed potatoes.

Kedgeree

you will need:

1 medium-sized	salt and pepper
smoked haddock	squeeze lemon juice
1½ oz. butter OR	¼ oz. butter
margarine	
¼ onion, finely chopped	**to garnish:**
6 oz. long-grain rice	chopped parsley
about ¾ pint boiling fish	
liquor	

1 Rinse the haddock and cut in pieces. Place in a pan with enough salted water to just cover and simmer until tender (about 10–15 minutes).

2 Strain the liquor and put aside for cooking the rice. Remove skin and bone from the cooked fish. Flake the flesh.

3 Melt the butter or margarine in a saucepan over low heat and add the onion. Sauté gently to soften (about 5 minutes).

4 Stir in the rice and the boiling fish liquor. Cover the pan and simmer very gently for 20–25 minutes or until the rice is tender and has absorbed all the liquid.

5 Add the fish flesh, salt and pepper to taste, lemon juice and the butter. Toss with a fork to mix, then turn into a hot serving dish. Garnish with chopped parsley and serve with hot buttered toast.

Stuffed peppers

you will need:

2 small green peppers
½ oz. butter OR margarine
1 rounded tablespoon fresh white breadcrumbs

for the filling:
2 rashers bacon

½ onion, finely chopped
1 8-oz. tin baked beans in tomato sauce
1 tablespoon tomato ketchup
1 teaspoon Worcestershire sauce
2 oz. grated Cheddar cheese

1 Slice the top off the green peppers, or cut in half across. Level the bases but do not cut through the pepper. Scoop out the seeds from the inside and discard. Melt the butter, stir in the breadcrumbs with a fork and set aside for the topping.
2 Plunge the peppers into boiling water and simmer 5 minutes. Drain and place open end up in a small baking dish. Set aside while preparing the filling.
3 Trim and chop the bacon rashers and fry gently until the fat runs. Add the onion and continue to cook until soft (about 5 minutes).
4 Add the baked beans, ketchup, Worcestershire sauce and cheese, and stir over low heat until melted and blended.
5 Spoon the bean filling into the peppers, top with buttered crumbs. Measure 1 tablespoon water in the dish round the base of the peppers, cover the baking or casserole dish with a lid, and place in the centre of a moderately hot oven (380°F. – Gas Mark 5). Cook for 40 minutes.
6 Serve peppers with creamed potatoes and fried mushrooms.

Variation

Meat stuffed peppers – follow the recipe above using 1 small tin minced beef instead of the baked beans and omit the tomato ketchup. Save the grated cheese and use to sprinkle over the filled peppers instead of the buttered crumbs.

Stuffed liver

you will need:

4–6 oz. calf's liver cut in two thick slices
seasoned flour

for the stuffing:
2 rounded tablespoons fresh white breadcrumbs
½ small onion, finely chopped

salt and pepper
pinch mixed herbs
1 teaspoon chopped parsley
1 oz. butter

2 bacon rashers
1 oz. lard for frying

1 Wipe the liver and coat both sides with seasoned flour. Set aside while preparing the stuffing.

2 Into a basin measure the breadcrumbs, onion, seasoning, herbs and parsley. Melt the butter and stir into the stuffing ingredients with a fork, mixing until blended and butter absorbed.
3 Pack the stuffing over each piece of liver and top with a bacon rasher.
4 Melt the dripping in a small roasting tin and add the prepared liver. Cover with a buttered paper, place in the centre of a moderate oven (355°F. – Gas Mark 4) and bake 1 hour.
5 Lift liver from the tin, and serve with grilled tomatoes and chipped potatoes.

Mustard pork rashers

you will need:

4 thick rashers fresh belly of pork
½ oz. butter OR margarine
1 level tablespoon flour
½ pint stock OR water plus stock cube

1 dessertspoon tomato purée
1 tablespoon mustard pickles, finely chopped
salt and pepper

1 Cut away the rind and roll the rashers tightly.
2 Place on the base of a greased casserole just big enough to keep them tightly rolled.
3 Melt the butter in a pan over low heat and stir in the flour. Gradually stir in the stock, beating well to make a smooth consistency, then add the tomato purée and the pickles.
4 Bring to boil, stirring well, season with salt and pepper and pour over the rashers.
5 Cover with a lid and place in the centre of a slow oven (335°F. – Gas Mark 3) and cook 1 hour.
6 Serve rolled rashers with sauce spooned over, and with creamed potatoes and baby Brussels sprouts.

Vegetable pila

you will need:

2 oz. butter OR margarine
1 onion, peeled and chopped
8 oz. brown rice (or use long grain rice, milled)

1 pint stock OR water
½ level teaspoon salt
8 oz. mushrooms, trimmed
8 oz. tomatoes
2–3 oz. grated Cheddar cheese

1 Melt 1 oz. of the butter in a frying pan and fry the onion gently until soft, takes about 5 minutes. Add the rice and fry for a further few moments.
2 Spoon the ingredients into a 1½ pint casserole or baking dish, and stir in the hot stock and salt. Cover with a lid and place in the centre of a moderate oven (355°F. – Gas Mark 4) and bake for 1 hour.

3 Meanwhile fry the mushrooms in remaining butter until tender.

4 Plunge the tomatoes into boiling water for 1 minute, drain and peel away the skins. Cut into quarters and remove the seeds.

5 Remove the lid from the hot, cooked rice and fold in the mushrooms and tomatoes. Sprinkle with grated cheese and serve with fried liver.

Osso buco

you will need:

1 veal hock (shin), cut Into 1-inch pieces	1 level teaspoon salt
seasoned flour	¼ level teaspoon pepper
1 medium onion	grated rind ½ lemon
1 large carrot	chopped parsley
2 tablespoons cooking oil	**for the rice:**
1 8-oz. tin tomatoes	4–6 oz. Patna rice
bouquet garni	little butter
¼ pint stock OR water plus stock cube	1 oz. grated Parmesan cheese

1 Toss the veal pieces in seasoned flour. Peel and finely slice the onion and carrot.

2 Heat the oil in a large saucepan and fry meat and vegetables gently until lightly browned.

3 Add the tomatoes, *bouquet garni*, stock and seasoning.

4 Cover with a lid and cook gently for 1½ hours or until tender. Remove the *bouquet garni* and add the grated lemon rind and a little chopped parsley.

5 Add the rice to plenty of boiling salted water, and boil quickly for 10 minutes. Drain and return to the hot saucepan, add a nut of butter, replace the lid on the pan, and allow the rice to steam dry for a few minutes.

6 Spoon the rice on to a hot serving platter, arrange veal and sauce over the top, sprinkle with grated cheese and serve.

Fish chowder

you will need:

1 tablespoon cooking oil	1 pint boiling water
2 onions, sliced	12 oz. fresh cod fillet
1 lb. potatoes, peeled and sliced	½ pint milk
1 level teaspoon salt	1 oz. butter OR margarine
pinch pepper	¼ pint single cream
	chopped parsley

1 Heat the oil in a large saucepan and sauté the onion gently until soft (about 10 minutes). Cover the pan to prevent browning.

2 Add the potatoes, seasoning and boiling water. Arrange the fish, skinned and cut into neat medium-sized pieces, on top.

3 Cover the pan and simmer gently 25–30 minutes, until the potatoes are tender.

4 Draw the pan off the heat and carefully lift out the fish pieces. Remove any bones and skin and flake the flesh. Replace fish flesh in the pan.

5 Bring the milk to the boil and add immediately with the butter or margarine and cream. Sprinkle with chopped parsley and serve in soup bowls with brown bread and butter.

Skate with caper sauce

you will need:

2 6-oz. portions skate wing	**for the caper sauce:**
½ lemon, sliced	2 oz. butter
½ level teaspoon salt	juice ½ lemon
	1 tablespoon capers
	1 tablespoon finely chopped parsley

1 Rinse the fish and place in a saucepan, cover with cold water and add lemon and salt.

2 Bring slowly to the boil, cover with a lid, poach gently for 15–20 minutes. Drain from hot liquid and arrange on warm serving platter.

3 Melt the butter in a saucepan and draw the pan off the heat, add the lemon juice and capers and the parsley.

4 Pour the caper sauce over the hot fish and serve with parsley, potatoes and green peas.

Spanish cod steaks

you will need:

2 tail-end cod cutlets	**for the sauce:**
salt and pepper	1 oz. butter OR margarine
1 tablespoon lemon juice	1 onion, peeled and sliced
¼ oz. butter	1 8-oz. tin tomatoes
	½ level teaspoon salt

1 Snip the fins away from the cod pieces, season and arrange the pieces in a buttered baking dish.

2 Add the lemon juice, dot with butter and cover with a buttered paper. Place in the centre of a moderate oven (355°F. – Gas Mark 4) and bake for 25 minutes.

3 Meanwhile prepare the sauce. Melt the butter in a small saucepan and sauté the onion until soft (about 8 minutes).

4 Stir in the tomatoes plus liquid from the tin and the salt. Bring to the boil and simmer gently covered with a lid for 20 minutes.

5 Pour the sauce over the fish steaks, cook for a further 5 minutes and then serve with chipped potatoes and grilled mushrooms.

Devilled fish grill

you will need:

2 tail-end cod cutlets	1 level teaspoon dry
1½ oz. butter OR	mustard
margarine	1 teaspoon anchovy
1 teaspoon chutney	essence (optional)
1 level teaspoon curry	salt and pepper
powder	

1 Snip the centre bone from the cutlets and cut away any fins. Arrange the cutlets in the grill pan. Spread with ½ oz. of the butter or margarine.
2 Place under a moderately hot grill at least 3 inches from the heat and cook for 3 minutes without turning.
3 Meanwhile combine the remaining butter or margarine, chutney, curry powder, mustard, anchovy essence and seasoning, and mix thoroughly.
4 Turn the fish and spread the uncooked side with the mixture. Return to the grill and continue cooking under moderate heat for 7–10 minutes or until the fish is cooked through.
5 Serve at once with sauté potatoes and green peas.

Braised pigeons

you will need:

2 pigeons, plucked and	pinch mixed dried
cleaned	herbs
seasoned flour	stock OR water plus
4 oz. streaky bacon	stock cube
8 oz. onions, sliced	1 teaspoon cornflour
8 oz. carrots, thinly	1 tablespoon water
sliced	salt and pepper

1 Wipe the pigeons and dredge with seasoned flour. Cut trimmed bacon into small pieces and fry until browned. Remove bacon and brown pigeons.
2 Place the prepared vegetables, herbs and bacon in a casserole dish. Arrange the pigeons on top and add enough stock to cover the vegetables.
3 Cover and place the casserole in the centre of a slow oven (355°F. – Gas Mark 3) and cook for 2–2½ hours.
4 Lift out the cooked pigeons and arrange in a serving dish with vegetables if liked. Strain the cooking liquor into a saucepan and reduce by boiling to about ¼ pint. Stir in the cornflour blended with the water. Re-boil, stirring until thickened. Check the seasoning and pour sauce over the pigeons.
5 Serve with grilled tomatoes and chipped potatoes and peas, and hand redcurrant jelly separately.

Cauliflower and bacon savoury

you will need:

1 small cauliflower	**for the cheese sauce:**
1 onion, chopped	1 oz. butter OR
4 bacon rashers	margarine
½ oz. butter OR	1 level tablespoon flour
margarine	¼ pint milk
2 oz. mushrooms,	salt and pepper
trimmed and sliced	2–3 oz. grated Cheddar
	cheese

1 Trim the cauliflower and break into sprigs of fairly even size. Wash well and cook in boiling salted water until tender (about 10 minutes).
2 Drain and arrange the sprigs in an ovenproof serving dish. Fry the onion and the trimmed and chopped bacon rashers in the fat until soft, then sprinkle over the cauliflower. Reserve the fat for frying the mushrooms later.
3 Melt the butter or margarine for the sauce in a saucepan over low heat. Stir in the flour and cook for 1 minute. Gradually beat in the milk, stirring all the time to get a smooth sauce.
4 Bring up to the boil, season and simmer 2–3 minutes. Stir in half the cheese and, when blended, pour over the prepared cauliflower.
5 Sprinkle with remaining cheese and place near the top of a hot oven (400°F. – Gas Mark 6) until heated through and browned on top.
6 Meanwhile fry the mushrooms in reserved fat and sprinkle over the cauliflower before serving.

Sausage curry

you will need:

½ oz. dripping OR	¼ pint stock OR water
vegetable shortening	plus stock cube
8 oz. chipolata	1 tablespoon mango
sausages	chutney
1 onion, sliced	1 teaspoon tomato
1 level tablespoon flour	purée
2 level tablespoons	1 oz. sultanas
curry powder	4–6 oz. long grain rice

1 Heat the fat and quickly fry the sausages until brown (about 4–5 minutes). Remove from the pan and keep hot.
2 Add the onion to the fat and fry gently until soft, then add the flour and curry powder and stir in the hot stock.
3 Bring up to the boil, add the chutney (with any large pieces chopped up), tomato purée, sultanas and sausages. Cover the pan and simmer gently for 20–25 minutes.
4 Sprinkle the rice into a pan of salted boiling water and cook rapidly for 10 minutes. Drain and return the rice to the hot pan and allow to steam dry for 5 minutes.
5 Serve the rice as a base and top with the sausages and curry sauce, and pass mango chutney separately.

Baked apples

you will need:

2 medium-sized sharp cooking apples
2-3 level tablespoons castor sugar
½ oz. butter
2 tablespoons water

1 Wash the apples and remove the core from the centre, keeping the apple whole. Run the tip of the knife blade round the centre of the apple to cut the skin. Place the apples together in a small baking or pie dish.
2 Fill the centre of each with sugar and top with butter.
3 Add the water to the dish and place in the centre of a moderate oven (355°F. – Gas Mark 4) and bake for 20-30 minutes or until the apples are puffy and quite soft.
4 Serve with the syrup from the baking dish spooned over and with fresh cream.

Variations

Baked apples with sultanas – follow the recipe above but fill the apples with a mixture of 2-3 level tablespoons brown sugar, a pinch ground cinnamon and 1 tablespoon of sultanas.
Baked apples with nuts – follow the recipe above, adding the finely grated rind of half a lemon to the sugar and a tablespoon of chopped mixed nuts. Fill and bake the apples as directed.

Banana custard

you will need:

2 level tablespoons custard powder
¼ pint milk
1 oz. castor sugar
2 bananas

1 In a mixing basin blend the custard powder with a little of the cold milk to make a thin paste.

2 Heat the remaining milk in a saucepan until almost boiling. Draw the pan off the heat and stir in the custard blend. Stir well and pour back into the milk saucepan.
3 Replace over the heat and bring up to the boil, stirring until thickened.
4 Add the sugar and the peeled and thinly sliced bananas. Pour the hot custard into two serving dishes and serve hot or cold with cream or top of the milk.

Bread and butter pudding

you will need:

2 slices buttered bread cut in cubes
1 level tablespoon sultanas
1 egg
¼ pint milk
1 oz. sugar
½ oz. butter

1 Place the bread cubes over the base of a buttered 1-pint baking dish, and sprinkle with the sultanas.
2 In a small basin, combine together the egg, milk and sugar. Whisk until lightly mixed, then strain over the bread cubes.
3 Add the butter in small pieces and set in a larger roasting tin with water to come 1 inch up the side of the dish.
4 Place in the centre of a moderate oven (355°F. – Gas Mark 4) and bake for 25-30 minutes until browned and set.

Variation

With meringue topping – for an alternative, separate the white from the egg and top the baked pudding with a meringue made as follows: whisk the white stiffly and fold in 1 oz. castor sugar. Spread the pudding with a little red jam, top with meringue and brown in the oven.

Cooking in a bed-sitter

Where cooking space is limited, recipes that can be prepared in one casserole dish or saucepan are the most suitable to use. These recipes each provide a complete meal because starch has been added in the form of rice, pasta, potato, pastry or dumplings. Vegetables are in some cases added too, or the recipe is served with a salad.

As you will see by the following recipes, cooking in a bed-sitter can produce many easy, new, trouble-free and exciting meals.

Kidney and rice casserole

you will need:

3 lamb's kidneys
½ oz. butter OR margarine
1 onion, sliced
seasoned flour
4 oz. long grain rice
1 8-oz. tin tomatoes
¼ pint stock OR water plus stock cube
salt and pepper

to garnish:
2 oz. grated Cheddar cheese

1 Trim away any fat and skin from the kidneys. Snip out the core and slice. *continued*

2 Melt the butter or margarine in a saucepan and fry the onion gently until soft (about 5 minutes). Roll the sliced kidneys in seasoned flour and add to the hot fat.

3 Fry quickly to brown then stir in the rice, tomatoes plus liquid from the tin, stock and seasoning.

4 Bring to the boil, cover and simmer gently for 20 minutes. When the rice is tender and liquid absorbed, draw the pan off the heat. Sprinkle with cheese and serve with warm crusty rolls and butter, or a tossed green salad.

Kidney hotpot

you will need:

4–5 lamb's kidneys	4 tablespoons stock
4 oz. back bacon	OR water plus stock
rashers	cube
1 onion, sliced	8 oz. potatoes, peeled
4 oz. mushrooms,	and cut in thin slices
trimmed and sliced	½ oz. butter
salt and pepper	

to garnish:
chopped parsley

1 Remove any fat and skin from the kidneys. Snip out the core and slice.

2 Trim and cut the bacon into pieces. In a greased 1½-pint pie dish, arrange layers of the sliced kidneys, bacon, onion and mushrooms, seasoning each layer with salt and pepper.

3 Add the stock and arrange the sliced potato over the top.

4 Cover with a greased paper and a lid. Place in the centre of a very moderate oven (355°F. – Gas Mark 4) and cook for 1½ hours.

5 Remove the paper and lid, dot the potatoes with a little butter and sprinkle with salt. Replace in the oven for a further ½ hour to finish cooking and to brown the potatoes.

6 Sprinkle with chopped parsley and serve.

Chicken paysanne

you will need:

2 chicken joints	4 oz. mushrooms,
seasoned flour	trimmed and sliced
1 oz. butter	8 oz. tomatoes, sliced
¼ pint stock OR water	salt and pepper
plus stock cube	1 tablespoon finely
	chopped parsley

1 Trim the chicken joints and roll in seasoned flour.

2 Fry in the hot butter to brown on both sides. Add the stock, cover with a lid and simmer for 45 minutes.

3 Push the chicken to one side of the pan, add the mushrooms, tomatoes, a good seasoning of salt and pepper and the parsley.

4 Cover and simmer for a further 15 minutes. Serve the chicken joints with the vegetables and chipped potatoes.

Potato sausages

you will need:

6 beef chipolata	1 teaspoon chopped
sausages	parsley
½ oz. dripping OR	1 egg, lightly beaten
vegetable shortening	toasted breadcrumbs
12 oz. potatoes	for coating
salt and pepper	2–3 oz. vegetable
½ oz. butter	shortening for frying

1 Separate the sausages and fry in the hot fat until cooked and golden brown (10–15 minutes).

2 Boil and mash the potatoes with plenty of seasoning. Add the butter, parsley and enough of the lightly beaten egg to bind mixture together.

3 Turn out on to a lightly floured working surface and divide into 6 portions. With lightly floured hands roll each portion of potato the same length as the sausage and then press round the sausage to wrap completely.

4 Dip first in remaining beaten egg and then in toasted breadcrumbs.

5 Fry in the hot fat until golden brown and heated through – about 6–8 minutes. Serve with bacon rashers if liked.

Tuna fish cakes

you will need:

1 7-oz. tin tuna fish	1 egg, lightly beaten
12 oz. potatoes	toasted breadcrumbs
salt and pepper	for coating
1 tablespoon finely	2–3 tablespoons oil for
chopped parsley	frying
¼ teaspoon Worcester	
sauce	

1 Drain the tuna fish from the tin and flake the flesh. Boil and mash the potatoes with plenty of seasoning.

2 Add the flaked tuna fish, parsley, Worcester sauce and sufficient lightly beaten egg to bind the mixture together. Mix thoroughly and then turn out on to a lightly floured working surface.

3 Divide the mixture into 4 portions, and shape each one into a round patty.

4 Dip first in the remaining beaten egg and then in the toasted breadcrumbs. Pat the coating on firmly and fry in the hot oil until golden brown and crisp on both sides. Serve with tossed salad.

Variation

Salmon fish cakes – follow the recipe above, using 1 (7 oz.) tin salmon in place of the tuna fish.

Potato cakes and bacon

you will need:

¼ pint (or 1 teacupful) mixed milk and water	salt and pepper
½ oz. butter	4 oz. grated cheese
2 oz. instant potato powder	2 oz. butter OR margarine for frying
1 small egg	4 bacon rashers

1 Bring the mixed milk and water and butter up to the boil.
2 Draw the pan off the heat and immediately stir in the instant potato powder. Beat until smooth and thick. Then beat in the egg, a seasoning of salt and pepper and the cheese.
3 Divide the mixture into 6 portions and with floured hands shape each into a round patty.
4 Fry in the hot butter or margarine until browned and then turn and brown the second side.
5 Add the trimmed bacon rashers to the pan, fry along with the potato cakes, and serve together.

Pork and rice

you will need:

8 oz. loin of pork	½ pint stock OR water plus stock cube
seasoned flour	salt and pepper
1 oz. lard OR dripping	1 small packet frozen peas, thawed
1 onion, chopped	
4 oz. long grain rice	

1 Cut the pork into ½-inch slices and coat with seasoned flour.
2 Heat the fat in a saucepan and quickly brown the pork slices. Lift the pork from the pan and add the onion to the hot fat.
3 Sauté the onion gently until soft (about 5 minutes). Drain away most of the hot fat, then stir in the rice and replace the meat in the pan.
4 Gradually stir in the hot stock, season and bring to the boil. Cover and simmer gently for 20 minutes, until the rice is tender and liquid absorbed.
5 Check seasoning and fold in the peas – heat through for a further 5 minutes. Serve with tossed salad.

Braised spare-rib pork chops

you will need:

2 spare-rib pork chops	¼ pint dry cider
1 tablespoon cooking oil	1 10-oz. tin new potatoes
1 onion, sliced	salt and pepper
2 sharp-flavoured apples, peeled and sliced	

1 Trim away rind and excess fat from the pork chops, and brown both sides of the chops quickly in the hot fat.
2 Lift from the pan and add the onion to the hot oil. Sauté for a few minutes, until beginning to soften, then add the apple, replace the chops and pour over the cider.
3 Cover with a lid and cook very gently for 1 hour, adding a little more dry cider if necessary. Towards the end of the cooking time, add the drained potatoes round the edge of the pan and allow to heat through.
4 Lift the potatoes and the chops from the pan and spoon on to a hot serving dish. Rub the onion and apple through a sieve to make a purée, season and serve spooned over the chops.

Skillet pork chop dinner

you will need:

2 pork chops	8 oz. potatoes, peeled and cut into small pieces
salt and pepper	
1 tablespoon cooking oil	1 small packet frozen peas
1 onion, sliced	
¼ pint stock OR water plus stock cube	**to garnish:**
4 oz. mushrooms, trimmed and sliced	chopped parsley

1 Trim away the rind and excess fat from the chops. Season and brown in the hot fat.
2 Lift the chops from the frying pan, add the onion to the hot oil, and sauté gently until soft (about 5 minutes), then stir in the hot stock.
3 Replace the chops in the pan and add the mushrooms. Cover and simmer gently for 30 minutes.
4 Add the potatoes, cover and continue cooking for a further 20 minutes. Five minutes before the cooking time is completed, add the peas.
5 Check the seasoning, sprinkle with chopped parsley and then serve the chops with the vegetables and gravy.

Pork chops with spaghetti

you will need:

2 pork chops	1 tablespoon lemon juice
salt and pepper	
1 small onion, finely chopped	¼ pint stock OR water plus stock cube
1 small green pepper, seeded and chopped	3–4 oz. spaghetti, broken into 1-inch lengths
1 8-oz. tin tomatoes	
1 teaspoon castor sugar	

1 Trim away the rind and excess fat from the chops. Place trimmings in a frying pan and heat

until the fat runs. Then discard the trimmings.

2 Season the chops and brown both sides in the hot fat. Add the onion and green pepper and sauté for a further few minutes.
3 Stir in the tomatoes plus liquid from the tin, sugar, lemon juice and stock. Bring to the boil and simmer for 30 minutes.
4 Add the spaghetti, cover and cook gently for a further 15 minutes.
5 Check the seasoning and serve hot.

Lamb chops with mushrooms

you will need:

2 lamb chops	2–3 tablespoons stock
seasoned flour	OR water plus stock
1 small onion, sliced	cube
4 oz. mushrooms,	salt and pepper
trimmed and sliced	1 small packet frozen
1 8-oz. tin tomatoes	peas, thawed

1 Trim the chops and dip in seasoned flour. Place in a casserole dish and add onion and mushrooms.
2 Add the tomatoes plus liquid from the tin, stock and season well.
3 Cover and place in the centre of a moderate oven (355°F. – Gas Mark 4) and bake 1 hour.
4 Add peas, cover and cook for a further 10 minutes.
5 Serve chops with sauce spooned over and with chipped potatoes.

Braised sausages

you will need:

½ oz. lard OR dripping	1 8-oz. tin tomatoes
8 oz. beef chipolata	salt and pepper
sausages	4 oz. long grain rice
1 onion, sliced	
8 oz. carrots, sliced	**to garnish:**
½ pint stock OR water	grated cheese
plus stock cube	

1 Heat the fat in a saucepan and quickly fry the sausages until brown. Turn frequently (about 5 minutes).
2 Lift the sausages from the pan and add the onion and carrots. Fry gently for 2–3 minutes to soften. Drain away all surplus fat and replace the sausages in the pan.
3 Add the stock and tomatoes plus liquid from the tin, and season.
4 Bring to the boil then sprinkle in the rice. Stir, cover and simmer for 15–20 minutes. Stir occasionally until the rice is tender and all the liquid absorbed. Remove the lid and continue cooking for 5 minutes.
5 Sprinkle with grated cheese and serve with brown bread and butter.

Hamburger stew

you will need:

8 oz. minced beef	8 oz. tomatoes
1 teaspoon salt	¼ pint stock OR water
pinch pepper	plus stock cube
½ onion, finely chopped	1 tablespoon tomato
or grated	ketchup
1 egg yolk	
seasoned flour	**to garnish:**
1 oz. butter OR	1 tablespoon chopped
margarine	parsley
4 oz. mushrooms,	
trimmed and sliced	

1 Prepare the meat balls by mixing together the minced beef, seasoning, onion and egg yolk. Divide into 6 portions and roll into neat balls (if you lightly oil your fingers it makes the job easier). Roll balls in seasoned flour.
2 Heat the butter or margarine in a heavy pan and add the meat balls. Cook gently and brown evenly. Transfer to a casserole dish. Add the mushrooms, plunge the tomatoes into boiling water for 1 minute, drain, remove skins, halve and add to the casserole.
3 Add 1 level tablespoon of the seasoned flour to the hot fat and stir over the heat until frothy and beginning to brown. Gradually stir in the stock and bring to the boil.
4 Draw the pan off the heat and add the tomato ketchup, check seasoning and strain over the contents of the casserole dish.
5 Cover with a lid, place in the centre of a very moderate oven (355°F. – Gas Mark 4) and cook for 45–50 minutes.
6 Sprinkle with chopped parsley and serve piping hot with crusty French bread and butter.

Beef hot pot

you will need:

12 oz.–1 lb. lean	1 level teaspoon made
braising steak	mustard
seasoned flour	¼ pint stock OR water
1 oz. dripping OR	plus stock cube
vegetable shortening	1 7-oz. tin whole kernel
4 small carrots, sliced	sweet corn, drained
3 medium potatoes,	
peeled and quartered	

1 Toss the meat in the seasoned flour and brown in the hot fat. Lift from the pan and place in a 1½ to 2-pint casserole dish.
2 Add the carrots, potatoes, mustard and stock to the meat. Season and cover with a lid.
3 Place in the centre of a moderate oven (335°F. – Gas Mark 3) and cook for 2–2½ hours.
4 Add the sweet corn and cook for a further 15 minutes, then serve with crusty French bread and butter.

Spaghetti supper

you will need:

salt	1 7-oz. tin corned beef
4 oz. spaghetti	4 oz. grated Cheddar
1 8-oz. tin tomatoes	cheese
1 small packet frozen	salt and pepper
or 5-oz. tin peas	

1 Bring a pan of salted water up to the boil. Add the spaghetti and cook for 10 minutes until soft. Drain and return the spaghetti to the hot pan.
2 Add the tomatoes plus liquid from the tin, peas, corned beef, cut into small pieces and the grated cheese.
3 Heat over a low flame, stirring gently, until thoroughly heated through. Season to taste with salt and pepper and serve hot.

Sausage dinner in a dish

you will need:

1 oz. butter OR	8 oz. beef or pork
margarine	chipolata sausages
½ small onion, finely	8 oz. tomatoes
chopped	1 small packet frozen
2–3 bacon rashers,	peas, thawed
trimmed and chopped	salt and pepper

1 In a large frying pan melt the butter or margarine and add the onion, bacon and sausages. Fry fairly quickly, browning the sausages.
2 Meanwhile, plunge the tomatoes into boiling water for 1 minute and peel off the skins. Cut into quarters and add to the sausages with the peas.
3 Season well; cover and simmer gently for 10–15 minutes.
4 Spoon the mixed cooked vegetables into the base of a hot serving dish and arrange the sausages on top. Serve with hot buttered toast.

Scalloped sausages

you will need:

8 oz. beef or pork	**for the cheese sauce:**
sausages	1 oz. butter OR
1 oz. lard OR dripping	margarine
1 onion, sliced	1 level tablespoon flour
3 medium potatoes,	¼ pint milk
peeled and thinly	salt and pepper
sliced	3 oz. Cheddar cheese,
salt and pepper	grated
pinch mixed herbs	½ teaspoon made
	mustard

1 Lightly brown the sausages in hot fat, then drain, slice in rounds and set aside. Add onions to pan and sauté gently until soft (about 5 minutes).
2 In the base of a 2-pint casserole or baking dish arrange a layer of potatoes, using one third of the slices. Top with half the sausages and onions, season and add herbs. Cover with another layer of potatoes, sausages, onions, herbs and seasoning, finishing with a layer of potato.
3 Prepare the cheese sauce. In a small saucepan melt the butter or margarine and stir in flour. Cook gently for 1 minute, then gradually stir in the milk, beating well to get a smooth sauce.
4 Bring to the boil, lower heat and cook gently for 5 minutes. Season well, then add 2 oz. grated cheese and mustard.
5 Stir until cheese has melted, then pour over the contents of casserole. Cover with a lid and place in the centre of a very moderate oven (355°F. – Gas Mark 4) and bake 1 hour.
6 Remove the lid, top with remaining cheese, brown under grill, and serve with grilled tomatoes.

Corned beef hash

you will need:

1 oz. dripping	4 oz. mashed potato
1 onion, peeled and	1 teaspoon chopped
sliced	parsley
1 7-oz. tin corned beef	salt and pepper

1 Heat the dripping and fry the onion over moderate heat until golden brown and soft.
2 Add the corned beef cut into small pieces, mashed potato, the parsley, and a seasoning of salt and pepper.
3 Mix thoroughly together, cover with a lid and leave over moderate heat for about ½ an hour or until the underneath is well browned.
4 Turn out on to a hot serving dish, cut into wedges and serve.

Spanish beef rice

you will need:

4 oz. long grain rice	1 green pepper, seeded
1 oz. butter OR	and finely chopped
margarine	1 rounded teaspoon
1 medium onion, sliced	castor sugar
8 oz. minced beef	
1 15-oz. tin tomatoes	**to garnish:**
1 level teaspoon salt	grated Parmesan
	cheese

1 Sprinkle the rice into a pan of boiling salted water and cook rapidly for 8 minutes. Drain and set aside.
2 Melt the butter or margarine in a saucepan, add the onion and fry over moderate heat until soft and golden brown. Add the minced beef and brown.
3 Stir in the tomatoes, salt, green pepper and sugar. Add the cooked drained rice, cover with a lid and simmer gently, stirring occasionally for 30 minutes.
4 Top with grated cheese and serve with crusty bread and butter.

Fried chicken Nanette

you will need:

2 chicken joints	1 7-oz. tin whole kernel
seasoned flour	sweet corn
2 oz. butter	4 tablespoons double
¼ onion, finely chopped	cream
4 button mushrooms,	salt and pepper
sliced	

1 Trim the chicken joints and dip in seasoned flour.
2 Heat the butter in a heavy frying pan and add the joints skin side down. Fry over moderate heat, turning occasionally until browned on all sides.
3 Add the onion and mushrooms and continue cooking gently for 25–30 minutes or until the chicken is tender.
4 Lift the chicken out on to a warm plate and add the drained corn and cream to the hot butter in the pan.
5 Stir gently until thoroughly hot but do not boil. Season to taste and spoon over the chicken joints. Serve with buttered brown bread or hot rolls.

Pork chops with apple

you will need:

2 pork chops	1 small onion
1 oz. butter	salt and pepper
2 sharp-flavoured	1 level teaspoon curry
cooking apples	powder

1 Trim the pork chops and add to the hot butter in a frying pan. Cook gently for 5–10 minutes turning to brown both sides.
2 Meanwhile peel, core and coarsely chop the apple and peel and chop the onion.
3 Lift the pork chops from the pan and set aside.
4 Add the mixed apple and onion to the hot butter along with a seasoning of salt and pepper and the curry powder. Fry gently stirring for 2–3 minutes.
5 Then replace the chops in the pan, piling the apple and onion mixture on top of the chops. Cover the pan with a lid and continue to cook gently for a further 20 minutes. Serve the chops with the apple and onion mixture.

Country casserole

you will need:

2 lamb chops	¼ pint stock OR water
salt and pepper	plus stock cube
1 onion, sliced	
8 oz. (about 3 medium)	**to garnish:**
potatoes	chopped parsley

1 Trim the chops and season lightly.
2 Place in a greased ovenproof casserole and cover with the prepared onion.
3 Peel and slice the potatoes across thinly. Arrange these neatly in the casserole to cover the contents.
4 Pour over the stock and cover with a lid.
5 Place in the centre of a moderate oven (355°F. – Gas Mark 4) and bake 1 hour. About 10 minutes before serving, uncover and place on the top shelf of the oven to brown the potatoes.
6 Sprinkle with chopped parsley and serve with buttered green beans.

Chicken-'n'-rice casserole

you will need:

2 chicken joints	1 small green pepper,
2 tablespoons cooking	seeded and sliced
oil	1 tin condensed beef
1 onion, finely chopped	consommé
2 bacon rashers	salt and pepper
4 oz. long grain rice	

1 Remove the skin from the chicken joints and lightly fry in the hot oil until browned on both sides. Lift the chicken from the pan and place in a casserole dish.
2 Add the onion and trimmed and chopped bacon rashers to the hot oil. Fry until lightly browned. Stir in the rice and green pepper and cook for a further 2–3 minutes.
3 Stir in the consommé, plus half a soup can of water and seasoning. Bring just to the boil and pour over the chicken joints.
4 Cover the casserole with a lid and place in the centre of a moderately hot oven (400°F. – Gas Mark 6) and bake 1 hour.
5 Serve with warm crusty bread, butter and tossed salad.

Scrambled egg rolls

you will need:

4 round soft rolls	4 tablespoons milk
4 slices of ham	2–3 oz. grated Cheddar
4 eggs	cheese
salt and pepper	1 oz. butter

1 Split the rolls and place a slice of ham in each. Wrap in foil and put to heat whilst cooking the eggs.
2 Lightly whisk the eggs, add a seasoning of salt and pepper, the milk and the grated cheese.
3 Melt the butter in a pan, add the egg mixture and stir over moderate heat until creamy and thick.
4 Spoon the mixture into the hot rolls and serve at once.

Apple snow

you will need:

1 5-oz. tin apple sauce
1 egg white
1 rounded tablespoon
  castor sugar
green colouring
few chopped walnuts

1 Empty the contents from the tin into a basin.
2 In a separate basin whisk the egg white until stiff and then gradually whisk in the sugar.
3 Fold into the apple purée, add a few drips of green colouring, and spoon into two individual serving dishes.
4 Sprinkle with chopped nuts.

Apple delight

Empty carton of yoghurt into a mixing basin; add grated rind and juice of 1 lemon, 1 oz. castor sugar and 1 oz. chopped walnuts. Coarsely chop or grate one eating apple into the mixture. Spoon into two individual glasses and decorate with a few black grapes.

Cream buns with hot chocolate sauce

you will need:

2 large cream-filled
  choux buns

for the sauce:
3 tablespoons milk
½ oz. butter
1 4-oz. packet
  chocolate chips OR
  plain chocolate

1 Place each bun on a dessert plate, and set aside.
2 Measure the milk and butter into a saucepan and bring to the boil over low heat.
3 Draw the pan off the heat and immediately add the chocolate chips, or chocolate broken in pieces. Stir until chocolate has melted and mixture is smooth.
4 Pour over the choux buns when ready to serve. Extra sauce may be re-heated over very low heat.

Pineapple sauté

Sauté canned pineapple slices in hot butter with a teaspoon of sugar added, turning often until they are golden brown. Serve topped with ice cream and a little sherry.

Pineapple delight

Lightly fry slices of madeira cake and slices of tinned pineapple in butter. Allow to heat through thoroughly, but do not brown. Serve warm cake topped with pineapple slices and pour over a little extra heated pineapple juice.

Banana pineapple cream

you will need:

1 banana
1 8-oz. tin pineapple
  pieces
¼ pint double cream
1 level tablespoon
  castor sugar
pinch ground
  cinnamon

1 Peel and slice the banana into 2 individual serving glasses.
2 Add the pineapple and juice, mix and set aside.
3 Just before serving, whip the cream until thick, stir in the sugar and ground cinnamon. Spoon over the banana and pineapple.

Quick chocolate rice

you will need:

1 small tin creamed
  rice
2 oz. plain chocolate,
  broken in pieces
few drops vanilla
  essence

1 Heat the creamed rice in a saucepan over very low heat, stirring all the time to prevent sticking.
2 Draw the pan off the heat and stir in the chocolate and a few drops of vanilla essence.
3 Spoon into 2 individual glass serving dishes and serve with single cream or top of the milk.

Butterscotch crunch

Prepare packet instant butterscotch pudding. When it is beginning to set, fold in ¼ pint whipped cream. Spoon into individual serving glasses, and top with crushed peanut brittle.

Sugary oranges

you will need:

2 sweet oranges
1 tablespoon soft
  brown sugar
2 scoops of ice cream

1 With a knife cut round the oranges to remove the peel and leave the fruit whole. Make sure all the white pith is cut away.
2 Slice across very thinly, removing any pips, and arrange the slices in two individual serving glasses. Sprinkle with brown sugar and set aside for 1 hour.
3 Just before serving top with the ice cream.

Glazed pears

Into glass dishes, spoon 2 tablespoons tinned creamed rice. Then top with pear halves, rounded sides up, and pour melted redcurrant jelly over top and sides of pears.

Pear surprise

Drain pears from a small tin. Place in a serving dish and fill centre of each pear half with thawed frozen raspberries. Decorate with whipped cream.

Fruit fool

Stir 2–3 tablespoons condensed milk into $\frac{1}{4}$ pint of unsweetened fruit purée (blackcurrant is especially delicious). Serve in individual glass dishes and hand round sponge fingers.

Hot spiced peach halves

Sprinkle drained canned peach halves with a little soft brown sugar mixed with a pinch of ground cinnamon. Dot each with a little butter and grill until hot and sugar has melted. Serve hot with cream.

Peach mallow

Fill tinned peach halves with crushed tinned pineapple. Top with snipped marshmallows, and put under hot grill until the marshmallows turn golden brown. Serve while hot.

Peaches de luxe

you will need:

2 large fresh peaches OR four canned peach halves	2 tablespoons brandy 1 tablespoon honey $\frac{1}{4}$ pint double cream

1 Plunge the fresh peaches into boiling water for 1 minute, then drain and peel away the skin. Slice in halves and remove the stone.
2 Arrange fresh or canned peach halves in 2 glass serving dishes, and pour a little of the brandy in the hollow of each.
3 Dribble over a little honey, top with the double cream whipped until thick and serve.

Peach slices in orange sauce

To the strained juice of a small tin peach slices, add heaped tablespoon of orange marmalade. Heat thoroughly, then pour over the fruit. Serve warm with whipped cream.

Fruit cocktail

you will need:

1 8-oz. tin fruit cocktail 1 banana, sliced	1 tablespoon sweet sherry OR brandy

1 Combine the fruit cocktail with the banana.
2 Stir in the sherry or brandy and serve with single cream.

Fruit and shortbread fingers

To any drained, tinned fruit syrup, add a little sherry or brandy. Pour over fruit and serve fruit topped with whipped cream; hand round shortbread fingers, separately.

Banana shortcake

you will need:

2 trifle sponge cakes 1 tablespoon sherry OR fruit juice 2 bananas	castor sugar for sweetening single cream for serving

1 Slice the sponge cakes in half and sprinkle liberally with sherry or fruit juice to soak.
2 Place the bottom half of each cake in an individual glass serving dish.
3 Peel and slice the bananas and arrange over the sponge cake base. Sprinkle with sugar and top with remaining cake halves.
4 Serve with single cream.

Quick creme brulée

Place seeded halved black grapes in a shallow baking dish. Cover with lightly whipped cream and chill until firm. Spread surface lightly with Demerara sugar. Grill under a preheated hot grill until sugar melts and caramelises. Serve at once.

Chocolate banana pudding

you will need:

$\frac{1}{2}$ packet chocolate instant pudding	1 banana, sliced chopped walnuts

1 Prepare half the contents of the packet of chocolate instant pudding following the instructions on the back of the packet (using half the ingredients).
2 When beginning to set, fold in the bananas. Pour quickly into 2 individual glass serving dishes.
3 Sprinkle with chopped nuts and set aside until ready to serve.

Chocolate creams

you will need:

2 chocolate cup cakes $\frac{1}{4}$ pint double cream	chopped walnuts

1 Remove any outer paper from the cakes and cut the cake down the centre. Arrange each cake in an individual glass serving dish.
2 Whip the cream until thick and spoon into the centre of each cake, sprinkle with chopped walnuts and serve.

Trifle

Line a dish with broken sponge fingers, and sprinkle with chopped glacé cherries. Pour in prepared instant pudding, and when it is set, decorate top with whipped cream and walnuts.

Fruit cream

Pour a prepared packet of instant dessert over either cut up orange segments or tinned pineapple chunks, and sliced bananas. Chill before serving.

Rice cream and raspberries

Into contents of small tin creamed rice fold in tinned or thawed, frozen raspberries. Sweeten if necessary, and serve with cream.

Ice cream melba

Top slices of jam swiss roll with ice cream and the following raspberry sauce. In a saucepan combine together tablespoon each of raspberry jam, castor sugar and water, plus juice of half a lemon. Bring to the boil, stir in well. Boil gently for 2–3 minutes, pour over the ice cream and serve.

Jelly jumble

Prepare half a lime or greengage jelly according to instructions on the packet. When set, whisk up with a fork and pile in individual serving glasses with drained fruit cocktail taken from a small can.

Supper in a hurry

There are days in every busy woman's life when the time available for preparing supper is very limited. For occasions like these it is a good idea to have a reasonable selection of tinned and package foods in your store cupboard. Chops or grills are also quickly prepared but can be more expensive.

Build up a stock of carefully selected items. Stewed beefsteak with tinned tomatoes and thickened with cornflour makes a tasty stew. Try 7½-oz. tin tuna fish or pink salmon for fish salads. Danish cooked ham or pork luncheon meat makes a delicious cold supper with potato salad.

For something a little more unusual, buy Spanish rice and add extra sautéed mushrooms or flaked fish. Tinned ravioli or cheese flaps, topped with plenty of extra grated cheese and browned under the grill, are delicious served with salad.

Always keep plenty of macaroni, spaghetti and long grain rice – they can form the basis of many quick and substantial meals. A jar of ready-grated cheese made up from leftover pieces is always useful – stored in a refrigerator. For quick desserts, a supply of instant whips and puddings can be turned into trifles and creams in no time. Tins of cream, evaporated milk and creamed rice are also handy.

Fried liver and bacon

you will need:

8 oz. calf's liver, thinly sliced	1 oz. lard OR dripping for frying
seasoned flour	4 bacon rashers

1 Coat the liver slices with seasoned flour on both sides, then add to the hot fat in the frying pan and fry over moderate heat for 2–3 minutes on each side – liver should be only just cooked.
2 Meanwhile, trim the bacon rashers and grill for about 1 minute on each side.
3 Lift the liver from the pan and top with the bacon. Serve with fried onion rings and sauté potatoes.

Wiener schnitzel

you will need:

2 veal escalopes	2–3 tablespoons oil for frying
1 egg	
salt and pepper	
2 oz. fresh white breadcrumbs	**to garnish:** butter lemon wedges

1 Ask the butcher to beat the escalopes out flat.
2 Crack the egg in a shallow dish, season and whisk lightly with a fork. *continued*

3 Trim the escalopes and dip first in the beaten egg and then in the breadcrumbs, patting to make a firm coating.

4 Heat the oil in a frying pan and add the escalopes. Fry gently for 2–3 minutes each side until brown, turning often to get even browning.

5 Lift from the hot oil and garnish with a pat of butter and lemon wedge. Serve with buttered potatoes and broccoli spears.

Kebabs and onion rice

you will need:

4 rashers back bacon	**for the onion rice:**
8 oz. calf's liver, cut in one slice	½ oz. butter
2 tomatoes	1 small onion, finely chopped
4 mushrooms	6 oz. long grain rice
salt and pepper	⅓ pint water
little oil for grilling	1 level teaspoon salt

1 Trim the bacon rashers and cut in halves. Cut the liver into cubes and roll each piece in a piece of bacon.

2 Thread halved tomatoes, liver, bacon and mushroom caps alternately on to skewers. Season and brush with oil.

3 Place under a moderate grill and cook for 10–15 minutes, turning to cook evenly.

4 Meanwhile prepare the onion rice. Melt the butter in a saucepan and add the onion. Sauté gently until soft (about 5 minutes).

5 Add rice, water, salt and bring to the boil. Stir once and then cover with a tight-fitting lid. Lower the heat and cook very gently for 15–20 minutes without removing the lid or stirring.

6 When grains are quite soft and liquid absorbed, turn into a hot serving dish, top with the grilled kebabs and serve at once, with a tossed green salad.

Variations

Lamb kebabs – trim away any fat from 12 oz. lamb neck fillet. Cut the meat into neat pieces and use in place of the liver in the recipe. Brush with oil, to which a few drops of Worcestershire sauce have been added. Grill for 15–20 minutes.

Pork kebabs – trim and cut 8 oz. pork fillet into neat pieces and use in place of the liver. Use a few chunks of tinned pineapple to replace the tomatoes. Brush with oil and grill for 15–20 minutes.

Trout with brown butter

you will need:

2 fresh trout	**to garnish:**
seasoned flour	little finely chopped
2 oz. butter for frying	parsley
juice ½ lemon	lemon wedges

1 Ask the fishmonger to remove the heads and clean out the trout.

2 Coat both sides in seasoned flour then place in the hot butter.

3 Fry fairly quickly to brown both sides, then lower the heat and cook gently, about 8–10 minutes in all. Turn to cook evenly.

4 Lift the cooked fish out on to a serving dish and keep warm.

5 Raise the heat under the pan and brown the butter, add the lemon juice and shake over the heat for a minute to mix. Then pour over the fish and sprinkle with chopped parsley.

6 Serve with wedges of lemon, creamed potatoes with snipped chives added, and grilled tomatoes.

Minted lamb chops

you will need:

2 lamb chops	1 teaspoon chopped
1 oz. butter	mint
1 teaspoon chopped parsley	salt and pepper

1 Trim the lamb chops and cut a slit 2 inches long from the outer edge to the bone, in each chop, to form a pocket.

2 Cream the butter and beat in the chopped parsley and mint.

3 Stuff the pockets with the mixture.

4 Season chops and place in the base of the grill pan under moderate heat. Baste with butter as it melts. Grill for 15–20 minutes, turning for even cooking.

5 Pour any butter from the pan over chops and serve with sauté potatoes and green peas.

Pineapple baked luncheon meat

you will need:

| 1 7-oz. tin pork luncheon meat | 2–3 cloves |
| 1 tablespoon Demerara sugar | 1 small 8-oz. tin pineapple rings |

1 Score the luncheon meat in a criss-cross fashion and sprinkle the sugar over the top. Stuff with cloves and place in a small baking dish.

2 Cut the pineapple rings into halves and arrange round the base of the meat loaf. Spoon over a little of the pineapple juice.

3 Place the dish in the centre of a moderate oven (355°F. – Gas Mark 4) and cook for 20 minutes, basting occasionally with the pineapple juice.

4 Lift from the dish and serve the luncheon meat sliced with pieces of pineapple, the juice spooned over and with new potatoes and green peas.

Sautéed pork fillet

you will need:

1 small pork fillet	fresh white bread-
seasoned flour	crumbs for coating
1 small egg	1 oz. butter
½ lemon	

1 Split the fillet in half lengthwise but do not cut right through. Trim away any fat or sinews and cut crossways into pieces.
2 Flatten each piece with a rolling pin, placing the meat between two squares of wetted greaseproof paper first – this way the meat doesn't stick and tear.
3 Coat the meat with seasoned flour, then dip in lightly beaten egg and then in the breadcrumbs. Fry in the butter over moderate heat for 8–10 minutes, turning for even browning. Squeeze over lemon juice.
4 Serve with parsley potatoes and grilled mushrooms.

Savoury fritters

you will need:

2 oz. self-raising flour	2 eggs
salt and pepper	milk to mix – see
1 7-oz. tin luncheon	recipe
meat	oil for shallow frying
½ onion	
1 teaspoon Worcester-	
shire sauce	

1 Sift the flour and seasoning into a mixing basin, using the coarse side of a grater, grate the luncheon meat and the onion into the basin.
2 Stir in the eggs, sauce and enough milk to mix to a fairly soft batter.
3 Fry tablespoons of the mixture in hot oil over a fairly high heat. When golden brown on one side turn over and cook the second. Makes about 6 fritters.
4 Serve hot with fried tomatoes and bacon rashers.

Cheese spaghetti omelet

you will need:

3 eggs	1 oz. butter for frying
¼ level teaspoon salt	2 oz. grated Cheddar
pinch pepper	cheese
1 8-oz. tin spaghetti	
with tomato and	
cheese sauce	

1 Mix together the egg yolks, salt, pepper and spaghetti.
2 Beat the egg whites until stiff and fold into the spaghetti.
3 Heat the butter in an omelet pan or small frying pan until quite hot, then pour in the omelet mixture.

4 Cook over moderate heat for 5–8 minutes, or until brown on the underside. Draw the pan off the heat and sprinkle the top with grated cheese.
5 Place under a hot grill until the cheese is melted and brown, then serve cut in halves with buttered toast or a salad.

Baked eggs and cheese

you will need:

3 tomatoes	1 oz. grated cheese
salt and pepper	½ oz. butter
2 eggs	

1 Plunge the tomatoes into boiling water for 1 minute. Drain the peel off the skins. Halve, scoop out the seeds and then slice the tomato flesh.
2 Butter a 1-pint pie or baking dish, arrange the tomato flesh over the base and season.
3 Crack the eggs over the tomato, season and sprinkle with the grated cheese.
4 Dot with butter and place in the centre of a very moderate oven (355°F. – Gas Mark 4) and bake for 20 minutes, or until the cheese has browned and the eggs set. Serve with hot buttered toast or chipped potatoes.

Tuna Spanish style

you will need:

1 tablespoon cooking	1 8-oz. tin tomatoes
oil	¼ pint water
1 small onion, sliced	salt and pepper
2 rounded tablespoons	2 oz. mushrooms,
pre-cooked rice	sliced
¼ green pepper, seeded	1 7-oz. tin tuna fish
and chopped	

1 Heat the oil in a saucepan and gently fry the onion until soft.
2 Stir in the rice, green pepper, tomatoes, water, plenty of seasoning and the mushrooms. Bring to the boil.
3 Cover the pan with a lid, reduce heat and cook gently, stirring occasionally, for 30 minutes.
4 Break the tuna fish into pieces and place over the top of the rice mixture. Cover, heat through for 5 minutes then serve.

Tuna 'n' cheese supper

you will need:

1 oz. butter or mar-	¼ teaspoon pepper
garine	¼ teaspoon made
1 rounded tablespoon	mustard
flour	2-3 oz. grated Cheddar
scant ½ pint milk	cheese
1 level teaspoon salt	1 7-oz. tin tuna fish

1 Melt the butter or margarine in a saucepan over moderate heat, and stir in the flour. Cook for 1 minute but do not brown. *continued*

2 Gradually add the milk, beating in a little at a time to get a really smooth sauce. Bring to the boil, and allow to cook gently for 2–3 minutes.

3 Add seasoning, mustard and the cheese and stir until the cheese has melted. Drain oil from the tin of tuna fish, flake the flesh and add to the cheese sauce in chunks. Stir only to blend, and allow to heat through.

4 Serve with hot buttered toast and grilled mushrooms.

Crispy pork fillet

you will need:

½ (about 8 oz.) small pork fillet	browned breadcrumbs
seasoned flour	2 oz. butter for frying
1 egg, lightly mixed	½ lemon

1 Trim away any fat from the outside of the fillet and cut the meat into 4 thick pieces.

2 Place each one, one at a time, cut side down between 2 sheets of wetted greaseproof paper (this prevents the meat sticking to the paper), and beat flat with a rolling pin.

3 Dip the flattened pieces of meat first in seasoned flour and then in beaten egg and lastly in breadcrumbs. Pat coating on firmly.

4 Heat the butter in a frying pan and add the meat. Fry gently for 5–6 minutes, turning to brown both sides evenly.

5 Drain from the pan, squeeze over the lemon juice and serve with creamed potatoes and green peas.

Quick corned beef supper

you will need:

1 tablespoon cooking oil	1 7-oz. tin corned beef
1 onion, sliced	½ oz. butter
1 small packet frozen peas, thawed	salt and pepper

1 Heat the oil in a saucepan and fry the onion gently until tender (about 10 minutes).

2 Draw the pan off the heat, add the peas and then arrange the corned beef, cut in slices, neatly on top. Season and add the butter in pieces.

3 Replace the pan over very low heat, cover and cook very gently for 15 minutes until the peas are tender and the meat heated through.

4 Serve with creamed potato. Pass horseradish sauce separately.

Eggs, beans and frankfurters

you will need:

1 7½-oz. tin baked beans with frankfurters	2 eggs
	salt and pepper

1 Empty the tin of beans and frankfurters into a buttered 1-pint pie or baking dish.

2 Make two hollows with a spoon, break an egg into each and season.

3 Place in the centre of a very moderate oven (355°F. – Gas Mark 4) for 15–20 minutes, until eggs are set.

4 Serve at once with fingers of hot buttered toast.

Quick sausage supper

you will need:

8 oz. pork chipolata sausages	1 7-oz. tin whole kernel sweet corn
1 onion, finely chopped	salt and pepper
1 apple, peeled, cored and chopped	

1 Arrange the sausages in a cold frying pan and place over low heat, turning constantly until the fat begins to run.

2 Add all the other ingredients, cover and cook over low heat for 20 minutes, stirring occasionally.

3 Serve with slices of hot buttered toast and grilled tomatoes.

Curry quickie

you will need:

3–4 bacon rashers	3 hard-boiled eggs
1 16-oz. tin curried beans	

1 Trim and chop the bacon rashers and fry in a saucepan until crisp.

2 Drain away the fat and add the beans. Heat through gently, stirring occasionally.

3 Shell the hard-boiled eggs and cut into quarters. Fold into the hot curried beans.

4 Serve with grilled tomatoes and fingers of hot buttered toast.

Smoked ham and pea soup with sausages

you will need:

1 packet smoked ham and pea soup	1 8-oz. tin cocktail sausages

1 Prepare the soup according to directions on the packet and bring to the boil.

2 Add drained sausages. Cover the pan and simmer very gently for 5 minutes, to heat through.

3 Serve the soup and sausages with crusty bread and butter.

Basic recipe for savoury omelet

you will need:

4 large eggs	4 teaspoons water
salt and pepper	1 oz. butter for frying

1 Break the eggs into a basin, season them and add the water. Mix the eggs thoroughly with a fork, but do not whisk.
2 Heat the butter in a 7–8-inch round frying pan over moderate heat until bubbling hot. Pour in the egg mixture all at once and tip the pan so that the mixture covers the whole of the base.
3 Using a fork, stir gently across the base of the pan; when the mixture begins to thicken, stop stirring and leave the omelet to set and brown on the underside. Take care the heat is not too high.
4 When the mixture is almost set, but still moist and creamy, loosen the edge of the omelet with a palette knife. Tipping the pan away from you, jerk slightly until the far edge of the omelet extends over the edge of the pan. Slide the palette knife underneath to help, if the omelet sticks at all.
5 If making a filled omelet (see below) add half of any filling at this stage.
6 Using a palette knife, fold over both edges of the omelet to the centre and pat down. Push the omelet right into the far side of the pan ready to turn out.
7 Tipping the pan over and towards you, allow the omelet to fall gently out on to the serving platter. The folded edge should be underneath. Spoon any remaining filling on top and serve immediately.

Fillings for omelets

Each of these fillings is enough for 1 omelet.

Herb filling

Finely chop about 1 tablespoon fresh parsley and chives. Stir into the egg mixture. If you've no fresh herbs, use 1 level teaspoon dried mixed herbs. Serve this omelet with a crisp green salad and fingers of hot buttered toast.

Cheese filling

Finely grate 3 oz. Cheddar or Parmesan cheese. Add most of it to the basic mixture, saving a little for the topping. Serve with grilled tomatoes and a green salad.

Bacon and onion filling

Trim and finely chop 3 rashers of bacon and finely chop 1 small onion. Sauté both these gently in a knob of butter until tender, but do not brown. Drain both from the fat and add to the basic mixture. Serve with extra grilled bacon rashers and sauté potatoes.

Tomato omelet

Dip 3 tomatoes quickly into boiling water and remove the skins. Halve and remove the seeds. Lightly chop the tomato flesh and add 1 level teaspoon mixed dried herbs. Sauté this mixture gently in 1 dessertspoon hot oil for 5 minutes. Spoon most of the mixture into the cooked omelet, saving a little for the topping. Serve with a little cooked buttered broccoli and chipped potatoes.

Potato omelet

This one is always a great favourite and is especially good if the potato is sautéed with a little chopped onion. Peel 2 medium potatoes and cut into dice. Place in a small pan, cover with cold water and bring to the boil. Remove from the heat and drain immediately. Add the hot, diced potato to a little hot butter in a small frying pan and sauté gently until cooked through and lightly browned (about 5 minutes). Drain from the fat and salt well. Spoon into the omelet. For a man-sized meal, serve with grilled sausages.

Mushroom omelet

Wash and chop 4 oz. mushrooms and sauté gently in 1 oz. butter for 2–3 minutes. Drain from the butter and spoon over the cooked omelet. Serve with grilled bacon and chipped potatoes or a salad.

Prawn omelet

Stir 4 oz. frozen prawns, thawed, into 3–4 tablespoons white sauce or cream. Heat thoroughly and then spoon over the cooked omelet. Serve with grilled mushrooms and a crisp salad of lettuce, cucumber and watercress.

Desserts in no time at all

Rio cream

Empty ½ packet of instant vanilla pudding mix into a small basin and add 1 level teaspoon instant coffee. Prepare the pudding as directed on the package and, when beginning to set, fold in ¼ pint whipped cream. Spoon into two individual serving dishes and chill well before serving.

Summer peaches

Drain the juice from an 8-oz. tin peach slices into a small saucepan. Add few drops vanilla essence and bring to the boil. Simmer gently for 5 minutes until the juice has thickened a little. Remove from the heat and add 1 small package frozen raspberries. Stir very gently until the fruit has thawed and *continued* heated through. Pour the hot sauce over the peaches and serve.

Rice-mallow cream

To the contents of 1 small tin creamed rice, add ¼ teaspoon vanilla essence, 4 marshmallows cut into small pieces (use wet scissors when snipping them). Fold in ¼ pint whipped cream, then pour into two individual serving dishes. Serve thoroughly chilled with sponge fingers and a few chopped nuts.

Apricot sundae

Into a small saucepan empty the contents of an 8-oz. tin apricots. Add 1 tablespoon orange marmalade and bring very gently to the boil. Simmer over a low heat only until the marmalade has dissolved and the apricots are hot then pour over ice cream and serve with sweet biscuits or wafers.

Ice-cream cake

Top slices of Swiss roll with coffee, chocolate or vanilla ice cream. To make quick chocolate sauce, dissolve 6 oz. granulated sugar in ¼ pint water over low heat, then bring to the boil and simmer for 1 minute. Remove from heat and whisk in 2 oz. cocoa powder. Whisk well until the sauce is quite smooth and allow to cool before pouring over the dessert.

Fresh strawberries

Serve the whole strawberries with separate small bowls of cultured or fresh cream and brown sugar. Dip the strawberries first in the cream and then in the brown sugar to eat.

Supper for two

Here are some ideas which I hope will help you to make evening meals varied and interesting. Whether you choose from this section or from one of the others, I believe the real secret of success lies in attractive presentation. Garnish with lemon if it's fish or veal dishes, or tomato slices with cheese recipes, or chopped parsley with meat. Experiment with new recipes as often as you can and remember to taste as you go along. It is much wiser to correct the seasoning while cooking than to discover that it is under-seasoned too late, when the meal is served.

Baked stuffed herrings

you will need:

2 large herrings	1 oz. shredded suet
	1 teaspoon lemon juice
for the stuffing:	1 teaspoon sugar
1 cooking apple, very finely chopped or grated	**to garnish:** lemon
1 heaped tablespoon breadcrumbs	parsley

1 Ask the fishmonger to gut the herrings from the head end (without slitting down the belly). Rinse the fish and scrape off the scales with a knife, working from the tail towards the head, then cut off heads.
2 Mix together all the ingredients for the stuffing.
3 Season the body cavity, pack with stuffing.
4 Place in a well-buttered dish, cover with a buttered paper and bake in a moderately hot oven (380°F. – Gas Mark 5) for about 20 minutes. Dish up, garnish with lemon and parsley and serve with sauté potatoes and grilled tomatoes.

Herrings in cider sauce

you will need:

2 fresh herrings	¼ pint dry cider OR use dry white wine
1 oz. butter OR margarine	salt and pepper
1 small onion, finely chopped	

1 Scrape the scales off the fish under running cold water. Remove the head, slit belly and clean out the inside. Wash thoroughly in cold water and trim away fins.
2 Melt the butter or margarine in a frying pan and gently sauté the onion until soft (about 5 minutes). Add the herrings and pour over the wine or cider.
3 Season and bring just to the boil. Cover with a lid and poach 8–10 minutes, turning the herrings once.
4 Lift out the cooked fish on to a hot serving dish and continue to boil the liquid until reduced by half.
5 Pour over the herring and serve with creamed potatoes and grilled tomatoes.

Fried sole and mushrooms

you will need:

2 small sole OR dabs seasoned flour	juice ¼ lemon
2 oz. butter	**to garnish:** chopped chives
2 oz. button mushrooms, sliced	

1 Ask the fishmonger to strip the skin from both sides of the fish, or skin them yourself, following instructions on page 92.

2 Trim away the fins with a pair of scissors. Dip both sides in seasoned flour and shake off the surplus.

3 Heat the butter in a frying pan, add the fish. Cook gently for about 5 minutes, turn and cook the other side. Increase the heat, if necessary, to brown the fish.

4 Remove the fish to a hot serving platter. Add the mushrooms to the hot butter in the pan and fry quickly for 2–3 minutes; add squeeze of lemon juice. Heat through thoroughly, then pour over the fish; sprinkle with chopped chives and serve with sautéed potatoes and green peas.

Grilled halibut with cheese

you will need:

2 halibut steaks, cut about 1 inch thick	**for the marinade:** 6 tablespoons salad oil
2 oz. grated Cheddar cheese	3 tablespoons vinegar
	1 level teaspoon salt
	½ level teaspoon pepper
to garnish:	juice 1 lemon
watercress	1 small onion, finely chopped

1 Trim the fish steaks and place in a shallow dish.

2 Mix the ingredients for the marinade well and pour over the fish. Leave to soak 1 hour, turning occasionally.

3 Pre-heat the grill, lay the fish on the greased grid in the pan and set under high heat.

4 Reduce heat slightly and after 2–3 minutes turn the fish. Grill for about 10 minutes in all.

5 Sprinkle the cheese over the cutlets and replace under the grill. Continue grilling until bubbling and brown.

6 Garnish with watercress and serve with grilled tomatoes and sauté potatoes.

Crab cakes

you will need:

8 oz. fresh (or 7½-oz. tin) crab meat	1 egg
1 small onion, finely chopped	½ level teaspoon salt
1 oz. butter OR margarine	½ level teaspoon mustard powder
2½ oz. (or 1 teacupful) fresh white bread-crumbs	1 tablespoon cream

1 Flake the crab meat, removing any sinews and fork up into a mixing basin. Sauté the onion in half the butter, until soft; takes about 5 minutes.

2 Draw the pan off the heat and add the white breadcrumbs, toss with a fork until the crumbs are buttery.

3 Add the crumbs to the crab meat along with the egg, salt, mustard powder and cream.

4 Heat the remaining butter in a frying pan. Drop spoonfuls of the mixture into the pan and fry until golden brown, turning them once.

5 Garnish the crab cakes with slices of lemon and serve with tossed salad and slices of brown bread and butter.

Fried plaice with lemon

you will need:

1 whole plaice	1 oz. vegetable fat for frying
salt and pepper	
1 small egg	
browned breadcrumbs	**to garnish:** wedges lemon

1 Ask the fishmonger to fillet the plaice for you.

2 Divide the fish into 4 fillets and remove the skin (see instructions, plaice with cheese sauce, page 92).

3 Dip the fish fillets first in lightly beaten and seasoned egg and then in browned breadcrumbs. Pat the coating on firmly.

4 Heat the fat in a large frying pan and, when hot, add the fillets and fry until golden brown on both sides. Takes about 6–8 minutes in all.

5 Garnish with lemon wedges and serve at once with sauté or chipped potatoes and grilled tomatoes.

Smoked fish eggs

you will need:

2 small golden cutlets	salt and pepper
¼ pint milk	2–3 oz. grated Cheddar cheese
½ oz. butter	
2 eggs	

1 Trim and cut away any fins and place the fish in a shallow pan. Add the milk, butter and cover with a lid. Bring to the boil and poach gently for 10 minutes.

2 Lift the fish from the milk on to a hot serving plate and keep warm.

3 Crack the eggs into a teacup and then tip into the hot milk. Poach gently until cooked, then lift out on to the fish.

4 Season the eggs with salt and pepper and sprinkle with grated cheese. Pass under a hot grill until bubbling hot and brown. Serve at once with hot buttered toast.

Chicken grill

you will need:

2 chicken joints	salt and pepper
2 oz. butter	2 rashers back bacon
½ lemon	

1 Wipe the chicken joints and trim away any loose skin. *continued*

2 Melt the butter and draw the pan off the heat. Rub the chicken joints over with the cut lemon, brush with melted butter and season.

3 Remove the grid from the grill pan and line the pan with kitchen foil, if liked, to catch the juice. Place the chicken joints in the pan skin side up, and cook under a moderate grill.

4 Cook the chicken for 10–15 minutes, then turn skin side down and cook for a further 10–20 minutes. Brush with melted fat several times during the cooking.

5 Trim the bacon rashers and cut into thin strips. Fry in melted butter and add a squeeze of lemon juice.

6 Pour the bacon and dressing over the grilled chicken joints and serve with chip potatoes and fried mushrooms.

Chicken and vegetable casserole

you will need:

2 chicken joints	1 soup tin water
1 oz. butter OR margarine	salt and pepper
1 onion, sliced	pinch mixed herbs
1 small green pepper, seeded and shredded	6 oz. long grain rice
	4 oz. mushrooms, trimmed and sliced
1 tin condensed cream of tomato soup	

1 Trim the chicken joints and brown quickly on both sides in the hot butter. Remove the joints to a fireproof casserole or baking dish.

2 Add the onion to the hot butter in the frying pan and cook gently for 5 minutes or until soft. Stir in the green pepper, tomato soup and water, seasoning and herbs.

3 Bring to the boil, simmer gently for 5 minutes.

4 Sprinkle the rice over the chicken in the casserole and pour over the sauce. Add the mushrooms and cover with a lid.

5 Place in the centre of a moderately hot oven (400°F. – Gas Mark 6) and cook for 1 hour. Stir occasionally to prevent rice sticking. When rice and chicken are both tender and cooked, serve hot with a tossed salad.

Beef sausage casserole

you will need:

½ oz. vegetable shortening	1 rounded teaspoon gravy thickening powder
2 onions, peeled and sliced	1 level tablespoon flour
8 oz. sausages	½ pint water
4 oz. mushrooms, trimmed and sliced	salt and pepper

1 Heat the fat and add the onions. Fry over moderate heat until soft – takes about 8 minutes.

2 Add the sausages and mushrooms and fry gently while preparing the gravy.

3 In a small cup or basin blend the gravy thickening powder and the flour with a little of the cold water to make a thin paste, then stir in remaining water.

4 Pour over the sausage and bring to the boil stirring gently.

5 Cover with a lid and allow to simmer gently for 20 minutes. Season with salt and pepper to taste and serve with mashed potato.

Chicken fricassée

you will need:

2 chicken joints	2 oz. button mushrooms, trimmed and sliced
1 onion, sliced	
1 bay leaf	
2½ oz. butter OR margarine	salt and pepper
	1 tablespoon cream
1 tablespoon flour	1 egg yolk
milk	6 oz. long grain rice

1 Place the chicken joints in a saucepan and add the onion and bay leaf. Cover with cold water and bring to the boil. Lower the heat and simmer very gently for 1 hour, or until tender.

2 Lift the joints from the cooking broth, strain liquid and reserve.

3 Melt 1 oz. of the butter in a saucepan and stir in the flour. Gradually stir in the chicken stock made up to ⅓ pint with milk, beating all the time to get a really smooth sauce. Bring to the boil, season well and simmer 2–3 minutes.

4 Sauté the mushrooms in the remaining butter over fairly high heat for 2–3 minutes. Add to the sauce with the chicken flesh and season.

5 Allow to heat through, then draw the pan off the heat and stir in the egg yolk blended with the cream.

6 Meanwhile cook the rice in boiling salted water until tender, drain and return to the hot pan, and allow to steam dry for 2–3 minutes.

7 Serve spooned over the rice.

Crunchy oven-fried chicken

you will need:

2 oz. butter OR margarine	2 chicken joints
pinch salt	2 teacups crisp corn flakes, crushed

1 Melt the butter or margarine and add salt.

2 Dip the chicken joints in this, one at a time, and then coat with the crushed cereal, patting firmly to form a good coating.

3 Place the joints in a shallow roasting or baking tin, skin side up and not touching each other.

4 Pour over any remaining butter and place in the centre of a moderate oven (355°F. – Gas Mark

4). Bake for 1 hour or until tender. During baking baste with the hot butter from the tin but do not turn the joints. If they brown too quickly, cover with a buttered paper.

5 Serve chicken joints hot with buttered potatoes and whole kernel sweet corn.

Chicken hunter style

you will need:

2 chicken joints	1 small bay leaf
seasoned flour	1 level teaspoon
1 oz. butter OR	castor sugar
margarine	4 oz. button mush-
1 onion, finely chopped	rooms
1 8-oz. tin tomatoes	½ oz. butter
¼ pint white wine OR	
chicken stock	**to garnish:**
salt and pepper	chopped parsley

1 Lightly coat the chicken joints with the seasoned flour and brown in the hot fat. Drain and place in a large saucepan.
2 Add the onion to the hot fat and fry gently until soft and golden brown.
3 Add to the chicken in the saucepan with the tomatoes and the liquid from the can, the wine or stock, seasoning, bay leaf and sugar.
4 Cover and simmer gently for 1 hour or until the joints are tender – test with the tip of a knife.
5 About 5 minutes before the cooking time is completed, remove the bay leaf and add the mushrooms lightly fried in the little butter.
6 Sprinkle with chopped parsley and serve either with plain boiled spaghetti or rice.

Stewed veal with mushrooms

you will need:

12 oz.–1 lb. veal fillet	½ soup can dry cider
OR stewing veal	salt and pepper
1 oz. butter	3 level teaspoons
small clove garlic	cornflour
2 oz. mushrooms,	water
trimmed and sliced	
½ level teaspoon	**to garnish:**
paprika	chopped parsley
1 tin condensed	
mushroom soup	

1 Trim away any fat or gristle from the veal and cut the meat into neat pieces. Fry in the hot butter to seal the meat but do not brown.
2 Rub the clove of garlic round the inside of the saucepan for flavour, then discard the clove. Drain the meat and place in the saucepan. Add the mushrooms to the hot butter, fry them gently, then sprinkle over the veal.
3 Add the paprika, mushroom soup, dry cider and seasoning. Bring to the boil, then cover with a lid, lower heat, simmer gently for 1¼–1½ hours.

4 Blend the cornflour with water to make a thin paste. Stir into the gravy and re-boil to thicken.
5 Check the seasoning and sprinkle with chopped parsley.
6 Serve with croquette or parsley potatoes and green peas.

Spaghetti with tomato sauce

you will need:

4 oz. spaghetti	1 level tablespoon flour
4 oz. grated Cheddar	1 lb. fresh tomatoes
cheese for serving	½ pint stock
	salt and pepper
for the tomato sauce:	1 2½-oz. tin tomato
1 oz. butter OR	purée
margarine	1 level teaspoon castor
1 onion, peeled and	sugar
chopped	1 tablespoon lemon
1 carrot, scraped and	juice
sliced	

1 First prepare the tomato sauce. Melt the butter in a saucepan and add the onion and carrot. Sauté gently for 5 minutes until onion is soft.
2 Stir in the flour and add the tomatoes, cut into quarters. Cook gently for 5 minutes to soften.
3 Stir in the stock, a seasoning of salt and pepper, the tomato purée, sugar and lemon juice. Bring up to the boil, cover with a lid and simmer for 30 minutes, gently.
4 Draw the pan off the heat and rub the sauce through a sieve and return to the saucepan. Check the seasoning and reheat gently.
5 Meanwhile, add the spaghetti to the pan of boiling, salted water and cook fairly rapidly for about 12 minutes or until tender.
6 Drain and place in a hot serving dish, top with tomato sauce and sprinkle with the grated cheese before serving.

Meat balls in mushroom sauce

you will need:

8 oz. lean steak	1 small egg
(braising or rump)	seasoned flour
1 onion, quartered	1 oz. lard OR dripping
1 clove garlic, crushed	for frying
with a little salt	1 tin condensed
(optional)	mushroom soup
¼ level teaspoon salt	
1 oz. grated Parmesan	**to garnish:**
cheese	chopped parsley

1 Trim away fat and mince the steak into a basin with the onion and garlic if used. Add salt and cheese and enough lightly beaten egg to bind the mixture together.
2 Divide into 8–10 portions, roll into neat balls with lightly oiled fingers. Roll in seasoned flour, then fry until brown in hot lard or dripping.
3 Drain away excess fat, stir in the soup plus a

soup can of water. Bring to the boil and simmer gently for 20–30 minutes, stirring occasionally.

4 Check seasoning, sprinkle with chopped parsley and serve with creamed potatoes and buttered beans.

Sausages with mushroom sauce

you will need:

8 oz. beef or pork chipolata sausages	1 oz. butter
1 onion, sliced	2 rounded teaspoons gravy powder
1 bay leaf	1 level tablespoon flour
¾ pint of stock OR water plus stock cube	water to mix
4 oz. button mushrooms	1 teaspoon tomato purée (optional)

1 Separate the sausages and place in a saucepan with the onion and bay leaf. Add the hot stock and bring to the boil.
2 Lower the heat, cover and simmer gently for 20 minutes.
3 Drain the sausages and keep warm. Strain stock and make up to ¾ pint with water if necessary.
4 Lightly sauté the mushrooms in butter.
5 Meanwhile blend the flour and gravy powder with enough water to make a thin paste. Stir in the hot stock and mix well.
6 Strain the stock into the pan with mushrooms and seasoning; bring to the boil stirring gently. Stir in the tomato purée, if used.
7 Add the sausages and heat through, check seasoning then serve with creamed potato and grilled tomatoes.

Veal Parmesan

you will need:

2 veal escalopes	1 oz. butter OR margarine
1 rounded tablespoon flour	Juice ½ lemon
1 oz. grated Parmesan cheese	
salt and pepper	**to garnish:** parsley sprigs

1 Ask the butcher to beat the escalopes out flat.
2 Measure the flour, cheese and seasoning on to a plate. Dip the veal in this to coat thoroughly.
3 Fry in the hot butter for 10 minutes until brown on both sides, turning occasionally for even browning. Lift the veal out on to a warm serving plate.
4 Add the lemon juice to the hot butter and shake over the heat to mix. Strain over the veal and garnish with a sprig of parsley.
5 Serve with parsley potatoes and grilled tomatoes.

Creamed sweetbreads

you will need:

8 oz. calf's sweet-breads	1 level tablespoon flour
¾ pint stock OR water plus stock cube	milk (to make up with reduced stock)
1 oz. butter OR margarine	salt and pepper

1 Soak the sweetbreads in salt water for 1 hour. Rinse and place in a saucepan with cold water to cover. Bring to the boil and drain.
2 Trim away any fat or loose tissue from the sweetbreads and replace in the saucepan, covered with the stock.
3 Bring to the boil and simmer gently for 45 minutes or until the sweetbreads are tender. Drain, reserving the stock, and set sweetbreads aside while preparing the sauce.
4 Melt the butter in a saucepan and stir in the flour. Cook gently for 1 minute but do not brown. Gradually stir in equal quantities milk and stock to make ½ pint, beating well all the time to get a really smooth sauce.
5 Bring to the boil and simmer gently for 2–3 minutes. Season well with salt and pepper and add the cooked sweetbreads. Heat through gently and thoroughly, then serve with grilled mushrooms and sauté potatoes.

Devilled steak

you will need:

12 oz. braising steak	1 carrot, thinly sliced
1 rounded tablespoon flour	1 8-oz. tin tomatoes
1 level dessertspoon mustard powder	1 teaspoon Worcester-shire sauce
salt and pepper	1 teaspoon brown sugar
2 oz. lard OR dripping	¼ pint stock OR water plus stock cube
1 onion, sliced	

1 Trim away any fat or gristle from the meat and cut into neat pieces.
2 Sift the flour, mustard and some of the seasoning on to a plate and coat pieces of meat thoroughly.
3 Melt the fat in a frying pan and fry the meat on all sides until well browned.
4 Meanwhile arrange the prepared onion and carrot in the base of a casserole dish. Add the browned meat; pour over the tomatoes and liquid, the Worcestershire sauce, sugar, seasoning and stock.
5 Cover with a lid and place in the centre of a slow oven (335°F. – Gas Mark 3) and cook for 2½ hours or until the meat is tender.
6 Serve with creamed potatoes and a green vegetable.

Lamb chops with pineapple

you will need:

2 lamb chops
salt and pepper
2 pineapple rings
pineapple juice

1 Trim the chops and season well.
2 Arrange in a casserole dish and top each one with a pineapple ring. Spoon over a little of the pineapple juice from the tin and cover.
3 Bake in the centre of a very moderate oven (355°F. – Gas Mark 4) for 1 hour.
4 Serve with creamed potatoes and grilled mushrooms.

Grilled bacon steaks and pineapple

you will need:

2 bacon steaks (back rashers cut ½ inch thick)
2 pineapple rings
oil OR melted butter

1 Cut away the rind from the bacon and soak for 1–2 hours in a little milk if the bacon is salty.
2 Arrange in the grill pan with the pineapple rings. Brush the lean part of the bacon and the pineapple with a little butter or oil.
3 Place under a hot grill at least 3 inches from the heat Grill for about 3 minutes under a high heat, then reduce heat and grill gently for a further 9–12 minutes, turning once.
4 Top with pineapple rings, spoon over dripping from the pan and serve with sauté potatoes and baked beans.

Mustard glazed gammon steak

you will need:

1 gammon steak, cut about 1 inch thick
1 tablespoon prepared mustard
2 oz. brown sugar

for the glaze:
1 tablespoon vinegar

1 Trim the rind from the gammon steak and leave to soak in cold water or milk for 1 hour.
2 Drain, pat dry and arrange on the grid in a grill pan. Blend together the ingredients for the glaze in a cup and brush a little over the meat.
3 Place under a moderate grill, at least 3 inches from the heat, and cook for about 10 minutes either side, turning once and brushing frequently with the mustard glaze.
4 Serve sliced with grilled mushrooms, green beans, and piped or creamed potato.

Liver and onion casserole

you will need:

8 oz. calf's liver, sliced
seasoned flour
2 oz. lard OR dripping
2 onions, finely chopped
4 oz. mushrooms, trimmed and sliced
¼ pint stock OR water plus stock cube

1 Trim the liver and coat both sides in seasoned flour.
2 Heat the fat and add the liver slices. Brown on both sides and then remove from the pan.
3 Add the onion to the hot fat, cover with a lid and fry gently until soft (about 5 minutes).
4 Place the liver in a casserole dish, add the onions and mushrooms and pour over the stock. Cover with a lid, place in the centre of a moderate oven (355°F. – Gas Mark 4) and cook for 30 minutes.
5 Serve with creamy mashed potato sprinkled with chopped chives or parsley.

Somerset scramble

you will need:

8 oz. potatoes
2 carrots
1 large onion, peeled and sliced
1 oz. butter OR margarine
8 oz. tomatoes
4 eggs
6 tablespoons milk
salt and pepper
½ level teaspoon mixed herbs

1 Peel the potatoes and scrape the carrots, and cut both into a neat small dice. Place in a saucepan, cover with cold, salted water and bring to the boil. Cook for 5 minutes, then drain.
2 Melt the margarine in a large frying pan and add the onion. Fry gently until soft, takes about 5 minutes.
3 Add the cooked potato and carrot. Plunge the tomatoes into boiling water for 1 minute, peel off the skins and cut in quarters, discard the pips. Add the tomato flesh to the saucepan.
4 Allow to heat through gently while preparing the eggs.
5 Crack the eggs into a mixing basin, add the milk, a good seasoning of salt and pepper and mixed herbs. Whisk together to mix them and pour over the hot vegetables in the frying pan. Cook over moderate heat, stirring with a fork, until the mixture begins to thicken.
6 Leave until browned on the underside, then pass under a grill for a few minutes to cook the top if necessary.
7 Sprinkle with chopped parsley and serve cut into half.

Spaghetti bolognese

you will need:

1–2 tablespoons oil	salt and pepper
8 oz. minced beef	pinch mixed herbs
1 onion, chopped	⅓ pint stock OR red
8 oz. fresh OR 1 8-oz.	wine
can tomatoes	4 oz. spaghetti
2 oz. mushrooms	nut butter
1 rounded teaspoon	grated Parmesan
flour	cheese

1 Heat the oil in a saucepan and add the mince. Fry gently to brown, then add the onion and cook a further few minutes.
2 Plunge fresh tomatoes into boiling water for 1 minute, drain, remove the skins and cut into quarters.
3 Peel and slice the mushrooms and add with the fresh or canned tomatoes to the ingredients in the pan.
4 Stir in the flour, salt, pepper, mixed herbs and the stock or wine, then bring to the boil.
5 Cover with a lid, lower the heat and cook gently for 20 minutes.
6 About 12 minutes before serving add the spaghetti slowly to a large pan of boiling salted water. Bring to the boil again and cook gently for 10 minutes or until strands of spaghetti break when pressed with the fingers.
7 Drain, place in a large hot serving dish and toss with a nut of butter. Serve the spaghetti and bolognese sauce separately – spoon the spaghetti on to the plate first and then the sauce over. Pass grated Parmesan cheese separately.

Beef curry

you will need:

12 oz. chuck steak	1 level tablespoon flour
6 oz. long grain rice	½ pint stock OR water
	plus stock cube
for the curry sauce:	1 dessertspoon chut-
1 oz. butter OR	ney
margarine	1 tablespoon soft
1 onion, chopped	brown sugar
¼ cooking apple, peeled	juice ½ lemon
and diced	1 oz. sultanas
2 level tablespoons	
curry powder	

1 Trim away any fat or gristle from the meat and cut into neat pieces. Place in a casserole dish and set aside while preparing the sauce.
2 Melt the butter or margarine in a saucepan and add the onion. Sauté gently for 3–5 minutes until soft and add the apple.
3 Stir in first the curry powder and flour and then add the stock. Bring to the boil, then add the chutney (having chopped any large pieces), sugar, lemon juice and sultanas. Cover with a lid and simmer gently for 5–10 minutes.

4 Pour over the prepared meat. Cover with a lid and place in the centre of a slow oven (300°F. – Gas Mark 2) and cook for 2 hours.
5 About 15 minutes before serving, sprinkle the washed rice into a pan with plenty of boiling water. Boil briskly for 10 minutes or until grains are soft. Strain, then turn into a hot dish and allow to steam dry in a warm oven for 5 minutes.
6 Serve the rice and curried ingredients separately. Spoon a bed of rice on to each plate and the curry over the top. Pass sweet chutney separately.

Variations

Egg curry – follow recipe above but after preparing the curry sauce cover with a lid and allow to cook gently for 30 minutes. Omit the meat, add three quartered hard-boiled eggs to the cooked sauce. Heat through for 5 minutes before serving.

Chicken curry – follow the recipe for Beef curry but after preparing the curry sauce cover with a lid and allow to cook gently for 30 minutes. Omit the meat and instead add the flesh from 2 chicken joints prepared as follows: place 2 chicken joints in a buttered baking dish or roasting tin, cover with a buttered paper and place in the centre of a moderate oven (355°F. – Gas Mark 4) and cook for 1 hour. Allow to cool for 5 minutes, then lift away flesh from the bones, cut into neat pieces and add to the curry sauce. Heat through for 5 minutes before serving.

Prawn curry – follow the recipe for Beef curry but after preparing the curry sauce, cover with a lid and allow to cook gently for 30 minutes. Omit the meat and instead add 8 oz. prepared prawns to the cooked sauce. Heat through for 5 minutes before serving.

Stuffed tomatoes

you will need:

4 large tomatoes	1 tablespoon chopped
1 onion, peeled and	parsley
chopped	2 oz. grated Cheddar
2 oz. butter OR	cheese
margarine	
2 oz. (or 1 level teacup-	
ful) fresh white	
breadcrumbs	

1 Wash the tomatoes and cut away a slice from the top. Using a teaspoon, scoop out the seeds and core from the centre and discard.
2 Place the tomato shells in a baking dish and add 1 tablespoon water.
3 Fry the onion in the butter over low heat until soft – takes about 5 minutes. Draw the pan off

the heat and using a fork stir in the breadcrumbs, parsley and cheese.

4 Spoon the filling back into the tomato shells, heaping the mixture into each one.
5 Place in the centre of a hot oven (400°F. – Gas Mark 6) and bake for 15 minutes. Serve with grilled chops or fried chicken joints.

Stuffed baked potatoes

you will need:

4 large potatoes	salt and pepper
1 oz. butter OR margarine	6 oz. grated Cheddar cheese
1 onion, peeled and chopped	

1 Scrub and then prick the potatoes all over and bake in the centre of a moderate oven (355°F. – Gas Mark 4) for about 1¼ hours or until soft.
2 Meanwhile fry the onion in the hot butter for 5–8 minutes or until quite soft.
3 Slash the cooked potatoes across the middle and scoop out the cooked insides into a mixing basin. Mix well with a good seasoning of salt and pepper and add the cooked onion and butter from the pan.
4 Stir in 4 oz. of the cheese and then spoon the potato filling back into the shells. Sprinkle with reserved cheese and grill until bubbling hot and browned. Serve at once with grilled sausages.

Banana fool

you will need:

2 bananas	2 level tablespoons custard powder
squeeze lemon juice	
¼ pint milk	1 oz. castor sugar

1 Mash the bananas in a basin with the lemon juice until soft.
2 Measure the milk into a saucepan. In another basin blend the custard powder with enough milk taken from the pan to make a thin paste.
3 Bring the milk to the boil and then stir into the blended custard powder. Return to the milk saucepan and bring to the boil stirring all the time.
4 Add the sugar and cook for 1 minute. Draw the pan off the heat and stir into the banana purée.
5 Pour into two individual serving dishes and serve cold with cream or top of the milk.

Variation

Apricot fool – drain the apricots from 1 (15 oz.) tin. Set juice aside and purée the fruit. Prepare the custard mixture as directed above and stir in the apricot purée. Serve cold – with the fruit syrup.

Junket

you will need:

½ pint milk	few drops of vanilla essence
1 level teaspoon castor sugar	little grated nutmeg
1 teaspoon rennet	

1 Measure the milk and sugar into a saucepan and heat gently until just blood heat.
2 Draw pan off heat and stir in rennet and vanilla essence. Pour at once into two individual glass serving dishes and leave in a warm corner of the kitchen until set.
3 Grate a little nutmeg on top and serve.

Queen of puddings

you will need:

2 rounded tablespoons fresh white bread-crumbs	½ oz. butter
	3 oz. castor sugar
finely grated rind ½ lemon	¼ pint milk
	1 egg
	little red jam

1 Measure the breadcrumbs, grated lemon rind, butter and half the sugar into a mixing basin.
2 Bring the milk almost to the boil over moderate heat, then pour on to the contents of the basin. Leave to soak for 10 minutes.
3 Add the egg yolk and then pour into a buttered ¾–1 pint baking dish.
4 Place in the centre of a moderate oven (355°F. – Gas Mark 4) and bake for 20–25 minutes or until set firm. Test in the centre.
5 Remove from the heat and spread the surface lightly with jam. If the jam is very solid, warm slightly first to make spreading easier.
6 Whisk the egg white until stiff, then add half the remaining sugar and whisk again. With a metal spoon fold in the rest of the sugar and spoon over the pudding.
7 Rough up the surface and place in a hot oven (400°F. – Gas Mark 6) for 3–5 minutes or until golden brown. Serve hot or chilled with fresh cream.

Banana cream

you will need:

2 bananas	**to decorate:**
1 carton yoghurt	finely chopped walnuts OR grated chocolate
2 oz. castor sugar	
juice ½ lemon	
¼ pint double cream	

1 Mash the bananas in a small basin, add the yoghurt, sugar and lemon juice and mix together.
2 Whisk the cream until thick and fold into the mixture.
3 Spoon into two serving glasses, top with finely chopped walnuts or grated chocolate and chill until ready to serve.

Old-fashioned chocolate pudding

you will need:

1 oz. cornflour
½ oz. cocoa powder
1½ oz. castor sugar
½ pint milk
few drops vanilla
   essence

to decorate:
chopped walnuts

1 Into a saucepan measure the cornflour, cocoa powder and castor sugar.
2 Stir to mix then blend in the milk. Place over a moderate heat and bring to the boil, stirring constantly until thickened. Simmer gently 1–2 minutes.
3 Draw the pan off the heat and add the vanilla essence.
4 Pour into 2 serving dishes, sprinkle with chopped nuts and serve with cream or top of the milk.

Pineapple fluff

you will need:

1 8-oz. tin pineapple
   rings
2 level tablespoons
   castor sugar
¼ oz. butter
juice ½ lemon

1 level tablespoon
   cornflour
2 teaspoons water
1 egg

to decorate:
few chopped walnuts

1 Drain the juice from the tin of pineapple and reserve. Chop the pineapple flesh coarsely and place in a saucepan with the juice, sugar, butter and lemon juice. Place over moderate heat and bring to the boil.
2 Meanwhile in a small basin, blend the cornflour with two teaspoons cold water to make a smooth paste.
3 Stir the blended cornflour into the pineapple mixture, re-boil and cook gently for 1 minute.
4 Draw the pan off the heat, allow to cool slightly and stir in the egg yolk.
5 Stiffly beat the egg white and fold in.
6 Spoon into two individual glass serving dishes, top with chopped nuts and chill until ready to serve.

Pineapple rice cream

you will need:

1 oz. short grain OR
   pudding rice
½ pint milk
1 level tablespoon
   castor sugar

1 egg, separated
few drops vanilla
   essence
1 8-oz. tin pineapple
   titbits

1 Wash the rice and remove any dark grains. Bring the milk to the boil in a saucepan and sprinkle in the rice. Cover with a lid, lower the heat and cook very gently, stirring occasionally, for 30 minutes or until soft and creamy.
2 Draw the pan off the heat and stir in the sugar, egg yolk and a little vanilla essence.
3 Set aside until cool, stirring occasionally.
4 Whip the egg white until stiff and fold into the mixture along with the drained pineapple pieces.
5 Spoon the pudding into two individual dishes and serve with a little of the pineapple juice poured over.

Apple charlotte

you will need:

2 oz. fresh white
   breadcrumbs
1 oz. shredded suet
1 level tablespoon
   castor sugar
8 oz. sharp-flavoured
   apples

1 oz. Demerara sugar
finely grated rind ¼
   lemon
1 teaspoon lemon juice
1 teaspoon honey OR
   syrup

1 Combine the breadcrumbs, suet and sugar and sprinkle half the mixture over the base of a buttered 1-pint pie dish.
2 Peel, core and grate the apples into a basin and add the sugar, lemon rind, juice and honey or syrup.
3 Mix together and spoon into the pie dish, top with remaining crumb mixture and press down lightly.
4 Place in the centre of a moderately hot oven (380°F. – Gas Mark 5) and bake for 35–40 minutes. Serve hot with cream.

Using up leftovers

I regard this as one of the most important sections of a cookery book. In order to cook economically for a small number, you must know how to use up the food that is left over. Cooked food from any dish need never be wasted and can always be combined with other foods, gravy or sauce to make a new recipe. There are a few important points to remember if the meals you prepare are going to be successful. Any food that is to be re-heated and used again must be used as soon as possible while still fresh. These ingredients that are already cooked should only be re-heated in the recipes and *not* cooked again. Remember, too, that re-heated food loses its flavour and so must be well seasoned or mixed with flavoured foods.

Re-heated foods need extra moisture otherwise they taste very dry, so combine them with a well-seasoned sauce, gravy or mayonnaise and then serve with freshly cooked vegetables or a salad.

Chicken and corn

you will need:

4 oz. long grain rice	salt and pepper
1 small packet frozen sweet corn	1 egg, lightly beaten toasted breadcrumbs
2 oz. butter	8 button mushrooms
8 oz. *leftover chicken and stuffing*	

1 Add the rice to a pan of boiling salted water and cook 5 minutes. Add the packet of sweet corn, re-boil and cook a further 5 minutes. Drain both together, toss with half the butter and keep hot.
2 Mince or finely chop the chicken flesh and mix with the stuffing and plenty of seasoning.
3 Stir in enough of the beaten egg to bind the mixture together. Turn out on to a working surface and divide into 4 portions.
4 Roll each portion into a ball and roll first in remaining beaten egg and then in breadcrumbs.
5 Fix chicken balls on 2 skewers alternately with the mushrooms. Brush with the remaining butter, melted, and grill under moderate heat for about 10 minutes turning to brown evenly.
6 Serve on skewers with rice and sweet corn.

Cream of vegetable soup

you will need:

8–10 oz. *cooked leftover vegetables*	1 oz. butter
¾ pint milk	1 rounded tablespoon flour
1 onion, sliced	salt and pepper

1 Mash or chop the cooked vegetables and place in a saucepan with the milk and onion.
2 Bring to the boil, lower heat and simmer gently for 20 minutes. Then rub through a sieve and re-heat.
3 Cream together the butter and flour and add to soup. Stir or whisk well until thickened, re-boil.
4 Simmer for 1–2 minutes, season well and serve.

Scalloped fish

you will need:

8 oz. *cooked white fish* (cod, turbot OR haddock)	salt and pepper
	1 teaspoon chopped parsley
1 oz. butter OR margarine	8 oz. cooked mashed potato
1 level tablespoon flour	melted butter
¾ pint milk	4 mushrooms

1 Flake the fish removing any bones and skin.
2 Melt the butter over low heat and stir in the flour. Cook gently for 1 minute, then gradually beat in the milk, stirring all the time to get a really smooth sauce.
3 Bring to the boil, season well and cook gently for 2–3 minutes.
4 Stir in the parsley, fold in the cooked fish and allow to heat through gently.
5 Pipe or fork a border of hot creamed potato round the edge of 2 individual scallop shells or a 1-pint baking dish. Spoon the hot fish mixture into the centre. Brush the potato border with melted butter and place high up in a hot oven (400°F. – Gas Mark 6) for 10 minutes to brown the potatoes.
6 Top with grilled mushrooms and serve.

Chicken and ham turnovers

you will need:

8 oz. flaky OR puff pastry	2–3 oz. cooked ham
	1 small tin cream of chicken soup
for the filling:	little milk
8 oz. *cooked leftover chicken*	

1 On a lightly floured working surface, roll out the pastry into a large square. Using a 3–4-inch round cutter stamp out 4 circles of pastry. Leave to stand while preparing the filling.
2 Remove any skin or gristle or bone from the chicken and ham and chop finely. Moisten with 1–2 tablespoons cream of chicken soup.
3 Spoon the chicken and ham filling into the centre of each pastry circle.
4 Moisten pastry edge on one half of each circle, fold over and press edges together. Prick the tops and place turnovers on a wet tray. Brush with a little milk, place fairly high up in a hot oven (425°F. – Gas Mark 7) and bake for 20 minutes, until risen and golden brown.
5 Serve hot with remaining chicken soup heated through and served as a sauce.

Meat sauce for spaghetti

you will need:

1 tablespoon cooking oil	1 level teaspoon castor sugar
½ onion, finely chopped	pinch of pepper
1 level tablespoon flour	8 oz. *cooked leftover meat, minced*
1 tin tomatoes	4 oz. spaghetti
¼ pint stock OR water plus stock cube	grated Parmesan cheese
1 small bay leaf	
½ level teaspoon salt	

1 Heat the oil in a saucepan and cook the onion gently until soft.
2 Stir in the flour and tomatoes plus liquid from the tin and stock. Add the bay leaf, salt, sugar and pepper. *continued*

3 Cover with a lid and simmer gently for 20 minutes. Remove the bay leaf, and stir in the minced meat. Cover and simmer for a further 10 minutes.

4 Meanwhile cook the spaghetti in boiling salted water for 10 minutes, until tender. Drain and spoon on to a hot plate.

5 Check the sauce for seasoning, pour over the spaghetti, sprinkle with grated cheese and serve.

Bacon and egg rice

you will need:

4 back bacon rashers	¼ pint milk
3–4 oz. *leftover cooked rice*	salt and pepper
2 hard-boiled eggs	2 oz. grated Cheddar cheese
1 oz. butter OR margarine	
1 level tablespoon flour	**to garnish:** chopped parsley

1 Trim the bacon rashers and fry until crisp. Crumble coarsely and add to the cooked rice and sliced hard-boiled egg. Set aside while preparing the sauce.

2 Melt the butter over low heat and stir in the flour. Cook gently for 1 minute, then gradually beat in the milk, stirring well all the time to get a really smooth sauce.

3 Bring to the boil and simmer for 2–3 minutes. Season well and stir in the cheese.

4 Carefully fold in the bacon, cooked rice and sliced egg. Allow to heat through for 5 minutes, then pile into a hot serving dish, sprinkle with chopped parsley and serve with hot buttered toast.

Beef fritters

you will need:

2 oz. plain flour	1 teaspoon Worcestershire sauce
salt and pepper	
1 egg made up to ¼ pint with milk	1 teaspoon chopped parsley
4 oz. *minced cooked meat (beef, lamb, pork, ham, bacon OR poultry)*	2–4 tablespoons oil for frying

1 Sift the flour and seasoning into a basin. Make a well in the centre.

2 Pour egg and milk into the centre of the flour. Using a wooden spoon, gradually stir the flour into the egg and milk, drawing in from the edge of the basin. Beat thoroughly, until it forms a thick creamy batter.

3 Stir in the minced meat, Worcestershire sauce and chopped parsley.

4 Heat the oil in a large frying pan and drop tablespoons of the fritter mixture into the hot oil. Fry over moderate heat until golden brown

on one side, then flip over and brown the second side.

5 Drain and serve with bacon rashers and green peas.

Chicken salad

you will need:

8 oz. *cooked leftover chicken*	2 tablespoons salad oil
2–3 stalks celery	½ onion, finely chopped
1 tablespoon lemon juice OR vinegar	2–3 tablespoons mayonnaise
salt and pepper	crisp lettuce leaves

1 Cut the cooked chicken into neat pieces, removing any skin or gristle. Place the chicken flesh in a basin with the scrubbed and chopped celery.

2 Combine the lemon juice or vinegar, seasoning, salad oil and chopped onion. Mix well and pour over the chicken and celery, then leave to soak for 1 hour.

3 Add the mayonnaise, mix thoroughly and heap the chicken salad on to the washed lettuce leaves; serve with buttered brown bread slices or hot jacket potatoes.

Blended gravy for re-heated meat dishes

you will need:

1 rounded tablespoon flour	salt and pepper
½ pint stock OR water plus stock cube OR vegetable cooking water	gravy browning

1 In a small basin, blend the flour to a smooth thin paste with a little of the stock. Then stir in remaining stock and blend well with it.

2 Strain into a saucepan and bring to the boil, stirring continuously until thickened and boiling.

3 Simmer for 3 minutes, season with salt and pepper and add a few drops of gravy browning.

4 Use as required for re-heating cooked meat, or poultry or adding to cooked meat dishes.

Potato and cheese pie

you will need:

½ lb. *cooked mashed potato* OR 1 lb. raw potatoes	2 oz. grated Cheddar cheese
2–3 tablespoons milk	salt and pepper

1 Mash the cooked potato (or peel, boil and mash 1 lb. potatoes).

2 Heat the milk in a saucepan and add the mashed potato and cheese, seasoning well. Mix well and heat through.

3 Spoon into a well-buttered 1–1½-pint pie dish, spread evenly and rough the top up with a fork.

4 Place high up in a moderately hot oven (380°F, – Gas Mark 5) and brown.

5 Serve at once with fried eggs or sausages.

Chicken pilaff

you will need:

1 tablespoon cooking oil	8 oz. *cooked leftover chicken*
1 small onion, finely chopped	4 oz. mushrooms, trimmed and sliced
2–3 bacon rashers	salt and pepper
4 oz. long grain rice	
½ pint chicken stock OR water plus stock cube	

1 Heat the oil in a medium-sized saucepan and fry the onion gently until soft (about 5 minutes).

2 Add the trimmed and chopped bacon rashers, and the rice, and stir over the heat for 1 minute. Stir in hot chicken stock, bring to the boil.

3 Lower the heat, cover the pan and cook gently, stirring occasionally for 20–25 minutes, or until the rice is tender and liquid absorbed.

4 Cut the chicken meat into neat cubes, discarding any bone, gristle or fat. About 5 minutes before cooking time is completed, fold the chicken and mushrooms into the rice. Cover and allow to finish cooking.

5 Fluff the rice up with a fork, check the seasoning and serve the chicken pilaff with hot buttered toast or a tossed green salad.

Creamed chicken in rice ring

you will need:

8 oz. *cooked leftover chicken*	¼ pint milk (or teacupful)
	salt and pepper
	1 egg yolk
for the sauce:	2 tablespoons cream
1 oz. butter OR margarine	6 oz. long grain rice
1 level tablespoon flour	1 small packet of frozen peas, thawed

1 Trim the chicken meat and cut neatly into pieces, set aside while preparing the sauce.

2 Melt the butter in the pan over low heat and stir in the flour. Cook gently for 1 minute. Gradually stir in the milk, beating well to get a really smooth sauce. Bring up to the boil, season well and cook for 2–3 minutes.

3 Draw the pan off the heat and stir in the egg yolk blended with the cream and chicken meat. Reheat very gently but do not boil.

4 Meanwhile, add the rice to a pan of boiling water and cook briskly for 10 minutes. Drain and return the rice to the hot pan to steam dry for a few moments and add the peas. Pack the mixture into a buttered ring mould and turn out immediately on to a serving plate. Spoon the chicken mixture into the centre and serve.

Potato cakes

you will need:

½ lb. *cooked leftover potato* OR 1 lb. raw potatoes	salt and pepper
	1 teaspoon finely chopped parsley
2 oz. butter	1 egg, lightly beaten
½ onion, finely chopped	toasted breadcrumbs

1 Mash the potato (or peel, boil and mash 1 lb. potatoes).

2 In a saucepan, melt ½ oz. butter and gently fry the onion until soft (about 5 minutes).

3 Add the cooked onion and butter to the mashed potato. Season well with salt and pepper, mix in the parsley and a little of the beaten egg to bind the mixture together.

4 Turn the mixture out on to a lightly floured working surface and divide into 4 portions. With lightly floured hands shape each portion into a patty.

5 Dip first in remaining beaten egg, then in toasted breadcrumbs.

6 Fry in remaining hot butter until golden brown, turning once. Serve at once with fried bacon rashers, eggs or sausages.

Lamb and rice savoury

you will need:

2 oz. long grain rice	1 8-oz. tin baked beans in tomato sauce
8 oz. *leftover roast lamb* (or use tinned meat)	salt and pepper
1 oz. butter OR margarine	2 slices hot buttered toast
2 tablespoons tomato ketchup	1 oz. grated Cheddar cheese

1 Add the rice to plenty of boiling salted water and cook rapidly for 8 minutes, then drain.

2 Meanwhile, cut the meat into dice and fry gently in the hot butter or margarine to warm through.

3 Stir in the cooked hot rice, tomato ketchup and baked beans. Season and re-heat thoroughly.

4 Spoon on to toast slices, sprinkle with grated cheese and serve.

Potted meat

you will need:

4 oz. bacon rashers	salt, pepper and pinch mace
8 oz. *cold cooked meat*	
½ small onion, quartered	2 teaspoons Worcestershire sauce
2 oz. butter	

1 Trim the bacon rashers and fry until very crisp. Pass the meat, onion and bacon through a mincer twice, into a basin.

2 Add the butter, seasoning, sauce and spice and beat well to mix. *continued*

3 Pack into a small jar or pâté dish and run a little extra melted butter over the top.

4 Store in a refrigerator and use spread on toast or in sandwiches – don't keep longer than 2–3 days.

Hampton pie

you will need:

6–8 oz. *leftover boiled bacon* OR 1 7-oz. tin corned beef
½ onion, finely chopped
1½ oz. butter OR margarine
1 teaspoon chopped parsley
1 tablespoon tomato ketchup
½ level teaspoon made mustard
1–2 tablespoons stock OR milk
12 oz.–1 lb. potatoes for the topping
salt and pepper

1 Mince the bacon (or break up the corned beef) and finely chop the onion.

2 Melt 1 oz. of the butter or margarine in a small pan and add the onion. Sauté gently 5 minutes until soft, then add the bacon (or corned beef), parsley, ketchup, mustard and stock or milk. Season and allow to heat through gently while preparing the topping.

3 Peel and boil the potatoes. Drain and mash with plenty of seasoning, remaining butter and a little milk.

4 Spoon the hot bacon mixture into the base of a 1-pint pie dish and top with the mashed potato roughed up with a fork.

5 Place near the top of a moderately hot oven (380°F. – Gas Mark 5) and bake for 30 minutes or until nicely browned. Serve at once with buttered broccoli spears.

Canneloni

you will need:

6 canneloni shells (allow 2–3 per person)
1 7-oz. tin tomato sauce
2–3 oz. grated Parmesan cheese

for the stuffing:
8 oz. *cooked meat, minced*
1 level tablespoon flour
½ small onion, finely chopped
1 teaspoon chopped parsley
salt and pepper
1 small egg, lightly mixed

1 Plunge the canneloni shells into boiling salted water and cook for 15–20 minutes, then drain and set aside.

2 Place the tomato sauce over low heat and leave to warm through gently. Meanwhile prepare the stuffing.

3 Mix the minced beef, flour, onion and parsley together. Season well and add enough egg to bind the mixture together. Stuff the cooked

canneloni shells with the mixture and arrange in a warm serving dish.

4 Pour over the hot tomato sauce, sprinkle with grated cheese and bake in the top of a hot oven (400°F. – Gas Mark 6) for a while until bubbling hot and the cheese is browned. Serve with crusty bread and butter.

French cheese sandwiches

you will need:

8 slices of bread
3–4 oz. cheese, cut in thin slices
little mustard OR chutney
2 large eggs
¼ pint milk
¼ level teaspoon salt
2–3 oz. butter OR margarine for frying

to garnish:
watercress

1 Using the bread, cheese and mustard or chutney, make up 4 sandwiches. Press well together and trim off the crusts.

2 Whisk the eggs, milk and salt lightly together and pour into a shallow pie plate or bowl.

3 Heat the butter or margarine in a frying pan until hot. Dip each sandwich both sides into the egg mixture, allowing the bread to soak up the liquid. Drain and place in the hot fat. Brown on both sides.

4 Lift from the pan, cut in halves and garnish with a sprig of watercress. Serve with sweet pickles or chutney.

Variation

With meat – similar sandwiches can be made using ham or leftover cooked bacon and a little mustard.

Stuffed onions

you will need:

1 large Spanish onion
salt
1 oz. butter OR margarine
chopped parsley to garnish

for the stuffing:
6 oz. *cold cooked meat, minced*
1 tablespoon tomato ketchup
1 heaped tablespoon fresh white bread-crumbs
salt and pepper

1 Peel the outer skins from the onion and place in a large pan. Cover with cold water, add a good pinch of salt and bring to the boil

2 Simmer gently for about 25–30 minutes, or until only just tender. Test by pushing a sharp skewer through to the centre – it should be soft, but quite firm.

3 Drain the onion from the water and cool for a few minutes. Cut through only to the centre – do not cut in half.

4 Separate the layers setting aside about 4 of the larger pieces.

5 Mince the small centre pieces of onion and add to the minced meat, tomato ketchup and the breadcrumbs. Season well, then spoon back into the 4 reserved onion shells and roll up.

6 In a saucepan brown the stuffed onions in the butter or margarine for 10–15 minutes turning to brown evenly.

7 Sprinkle with chopped parsley and serve with mashed potato and brown gravy.

Variation

With corned beef – follow the recipe above but use 1 8-oz. tin corned beef in place of the cold cooked meat. Finely chop the onion in the recipe and mix into the corned beef.

Cheese vegetables

you will need:

approximately 8 oz. cooked leftover vegetables	1 level tablespoon flour
	⅛ pint milk
knob of butter	salt and pepper
	3 oz. grated **Cheddar** cheese

for the cheese sauce:
1 oz. butter OR margarine

1 Cut the cooked vegetables into suitably sized small pieces, and place in a buttered baking dish.

2 Melt the margarine or butter for the sauce over a low heat and stir in the flour. Cook gently for 1 minute.

3 Gradually beat in the milk, stirring well all the time to get a really smooth sauce. Bring to the boil, season well and simmer for 1–2 minutes.

4 Stir in 2 oz. of the grated cheese and when melted pour over the cooked vegetables. Sprinkle with the remaining cheese, place in the centre of a moderate oven (355°F. – Gas Mark 4) and heat through for 20 minutes.

5 Pass under a hot grill to brown and serve.

Vegetable hash

you will need:

cooked potato and vegetables	2–3 oz. grated cheese
salt and pepper	extra ingredients for serving
butter	

1 Mash together any leftover potato and vegetables and season to taste.

2 Well butter a small frying pan and with lightly floured hands press the potato mixture into the pan.

3 Lightly sauté the underneath over moderate heat until lightly browned and the mixture warmed through.

4 Sprinkle with the grated cheese and place under a hot grill until bubbling and browned.

5 Cut into wedges and serve with **grilled tomatoes** and grilled bacon or fried eggs.

Melba toast

you will need:

day old bread slices
(preferably from a sliced loaf)

1 Toast the bread slices on one side and, while still hot, trim away any crusts from the slices. Split toast into two slices and cut each half across into triangle.

2 Toast the untoasted sides (the toast at this point will curl up a little), then allow to cool.

3 Store in a tightly lidded tin. Serve with hot soup or cheese tray.

Chocolate custard cream

you will need:

2 egg yolks	1–2 drops vanilla essence
1 level tablespoon castor sugar	2 oz. plain chocolate, broken in pieces
1 level teaspoon corn-flour	
¼ pint milk	**to decorate:**
	chopped walnuts

1 In a small basin, combine together the egg yolks, sugar and cornflour. Gradually stir in the cold milk and then strain into a small saucepan.

2 Cook over low heat stirring until the custard has thickened and just comes to the boil.

3 Draw the pan off the heat; add the vanilla essence and broken chocolate. Stir until blended and smooth then pour into two individual glasses or serving dishes.

4 Sprinkle with chopped walnuts and chill until ready to serve. Serve with fresh cream or top of the milk.

Cinnamon toast

you will need:

day old bread slices	**for the cinnamon sugar:**
butter	1 level tablespoon ground cinnamon
	3 level tablespoons castor sugar

1 Toast the bread slices and spread with butter while hot.

2 Make cinnamon sugar by mixing together the ground cinnamon and castor sugar (1 part cinnamon to 3 parts sugar) you may find it useful to make up ahead the sugar and store in a sugar sifter ready for use. Sprinkle on to hot toast.

3 Cut the toast in fingers and serve.

Sunday trifles

you will need:

pieces of leftover plain sponge
little tinned fruit juice OR sherry

½ pint milk
finely grated rind and juice ½ lemon
1 oz. castor sugar

toasted flaked almonds

for the lemon custard:
2 level tablespoons custard powder

1 Break the pieces of sponge cake into the base of two individual glass serving dishes. Sprinkle over fruit juice or sherry to moisten.
2 In a small basin blend the custard powder with a little of the milk to make a thin smooth paste.
3 Pour the remaining milk into a saucepan and bring back almost to the boil. Stir into the custard powder blend, mix well and pour back into the milk saucepan.
4 Add the grated lemon rind and stir over moderate heat until thickened and boiling. Draw the pan off the heat and stir in the sugar and lemon juice.
5 Allow to cool a little, stirring occasionally, then pour over the sponge cake. Sprinkle with toasted almonds and chill until ready to use. Serve with fresh cream.

Chocolate truffle cakes

you will need:

4 oz. *stale cake crumbs*
4 oz. castor sugar
4 oz. ground almonds
2 tablespoons hot apricot jam

for the chocolate icing:
2 oz. plain chocolate
3 tablespoons water
4 oz. icing sugar, sieved
vanilla essence
chopped walnuts OR chocolate vermicelli

1 Rub the cake pieces through a coarse sieve to make the crumbs. Add the sugar, ground almonds and enough hot apricot jam to bind the mixture together.
2 Divide the mixture into 12 portions about the size of a large walnut. Shape each one into a round ball. Leave until quite cold and set firm.
3 To make the chocolate icing, melt the chocolate in the water over a low heat, draw the pan off the heat and stir in the icing sugar.
4 Add the vanilla essence and stir well until the icing is quite smooth.
5 Dip the cakes in icing and roll in the finely chopped walnuts or chocolate vermicelli. Place in paper cases, and leave to set.

Tutti frutti rice cream

you will need:

¼ pint double cream
2 tablespoons castor sugar
1 8-oz. tin fruit salad

1 teacupful cooked plain boiled rice
1 tablespoon finely chopped walnuts

1 Whip the cream until just beginning to thicken. Add the sugar and beat until thick.
2 Drain the fruit salad, cut into large pieces and add to the mixture Add rice and mix.
3 Spoon into two individual serving glasses and top with the nuts.

Fruit sponge pudding

you will need:

about 1 *teacup leftover sponge cake*
1 tablespoon stewed fresh OR tinned fruit OR sultanas

1 tablespoon sugar
1 egg
¼ pint milk
few drops vanilla essence

1 Break the sponge cake over the base of a buttered ½-pint baking dish. Add the fruit or sultanas.
2 Measure the sugar, egg and milk into a small basin. Whisk lightly to mix. Then add the vanilla essence.
3 Strain over the contents of the baking dish. Set in a baking tin with water to come 1 inch up the sides of the dish.
4 Place in the centre of a slow oven (335°F. – Gas Mark 3) and bake for 24–30 minutes or until set firm.
5 Sprinkle with sugar and serve warm with fresh cream.

Snacks after 10 p.m.

If you work it out you'll probably be amazed just how often an 'after-ten' snack is called for. Here are some quick-to-prepare snacks, all tasty and easy to serve. I think you'll find something for every 'after ten' occasion.

Open sandwiches

Arrange a colourful selection of toppings on buttered rye or brown-bread slices. Combine foods that go well together, be generous with the toppings and then garnish attractively. Serve with a knife and fork – these are usually bulky and awkward to eat with the fingers. Here are some suggestions for toppings.

● A base of crisp lettuce topped with peeled **prawns and mayonnaise**, garnished with a pinch of paprika and a wedge of lemon.

● **Thin slices of ham,** topped with lightly scrambled egg and a garnish of watercress

● **Sliced cooked meat,** topped with potato salad (diced cooked potato in mayonnaise), and garnished with chopped chives.

● **Sliced salami,** topped with onion rings (marinated in a little vinegar for a few hours first) and gherkin fans.

● **Tinned salmon,** blended with mayonnaise, and topped with sliced cucumber and lemon wedges.

● **Liver pâté** topped with sliced sautéed mushrooms, and a rasher of crisply fried bacon.

● **Thinly sliced ham or tongue,** topped with slices of hard-boiled egg and tomato and with a sprig of watercress.

Cheese pudding

you will need:

¾ pint milk	salt and pepper
½ onion	pinch cayenne
1 small bay leaf	little butter OR
few parsley stalks	margarine
4 oz. fresh white	
breadcrumbs	**to garnish:**
2 eggs	watercress and sliced
4 oz. grated Cheddar	tomatoes
cheese	

1 Bring the milk, onion, bay leaf and parsley stalks to the boil; draw off the heat and leave to infuse for 10–15 minutes.
2 Strain over the breadcrumbs and leave to soak for 30 minutes. Add the lightly beaten eggs, half the cheese and plenty of seasoning to the mixture.
3 Pour into a well-buttered pie dish and sprinkle with the remaining cheese and a few small pieces of butter or margarine. Place in the centre of a moderately hot oven (400°F. – Gas Mark 6) and bake for 30 minutes or until set and golden brown.
4 Garnish with watercress and slices of tomato and serve with hot buttered toast.

Sunnyside eggs on toast

you will need:

2 slices white bread	salt and pepper
butter OR margarine	2 oz. grated cheese
1 7-oz. tin whole kernel	
sweet corn	**to garnish:**
2 eggs	watercress

1 Toast the slices of bread on one side only.
2 Spread *untoasted* sides with butter or margarine and top with drained heated sweet corn.
3 Poach the eggs in simmering salted water until softly cooked, drain and arrange each on top of the sweet corn. Season.
4 Sprinkle liberally with grated cheese and place under a hot grill until bubbling hot and browned.
5 Garnish with a sprig of watercress and serve.

Tuna supper toasts

you will need:

3 slices bread	1 tablespoon
1 7-oz. tin tuna fish	mayonnaise
1 tablespoon tomato	1 tablespoon finely
ketchup	chopped onion
	3 thin slices cheese

1 Toast the bread on one side only.
2 Meanwhile drain the tuna fish and flake into a basin. Mash with a fork then add the tomato ketchup, mayonnaise and onion.
3 Mix well and spread over the untoasted sides of the bread slices. Top the tuna mixture with a cheese slice and grill under moderate heat until bubbling hot and browned.
4 Cut slices in half and serve at once.

Egg in a bun

you will need:

2 soft rolls	salt and pepper
1 3-oz. tin devilled	
ham	**to garnish:**
little made mustard	watercress
2 small eggs	

1 Split the soft rolls in halves and grill until brown.
2 Meanwhile mix the devilled ham with a little mustard to taste. Spoon half the mixture into the base of each roll and spread over the surface, forming a ring round the edge and a hollow in the centre.
3 Crack an egg into the middle of each ring, and season with salt and pepper.
4 Arrange the buns on a baking tray and place in the centre of a moderate oven (355°F. – Gas Mark 4) and bake for 12–15 minutes, or until the egg has set.
5 Serve covered with top half of the bun and garnish with sprig of watercress.

Crab sandwich bake

you will need:

4 slices bread	salt and pepper
butter	2 eggs
1 3½-oz. tin crabmeat	¼ pint milk
2 oz. Cheddar cheese, grated	

1 Trim the crusts from the bread and butter slices lightly on one side.
2 Remove sinews and flake crab flesh.
3 Sandwich bread with the crab flesh and grated cheese.
4 Cut the sandwiches into quarters and arrange them in a shallow buttered baking dish.
5 Beat together the eggs and milk, season well and pour over the sandwiches.
6 Place in the centre of a moderate oven (355°F. – Gas Mark 4) and bake for 30 minutes until set and golden brown. Serve hot with sweet pickles.

Saturday night bap

you will need:

4 bap rolls	1 rounded teaspoon
1 medium green pepper	French mustard
4 rashers streaky bacon	2 rounded tablespoons
2 hard-boiled eggs	tomato ketchup
1 small onion	4 thin slices Cheddar
1 slice day-old bread	cheese

1 Split the baps and set aside while preparing the filling.
2 Halve and seed the green pepper. Cook bacon until crisp. Finely chop or mince the eggs, bacon, onion, green pepper, and bread. Blend with the mustard and tomato ketchup, and place in a saucepan. Over low heat, warm the contents of the pan gently.
3 Meanwhile lightly toast the baps. Heap the warm filling on the bottom halves of the toasted baps, top each with a slice of cheese and grill slowly until the cheese begins to melt.
4 Top with remaining bap halves and serve at once with a green salad and whole tomatoes.

Mushroom eggs Benedict

you will need:

2 slices bread	1 tin condensed cream
butter	of mushroom soup
2 thin slices ham	½ soup can water
2 eggs	little chopped parsley
salt and pepper	

1 Toast the bread on both sides and butter while hot.
2 Top each slice with ham and arrange on a serving plate.

3 Lightly poach the eggs in salted simmering water, drain and arrange on top of the ham. Season with salt and pepper.
4 Meanwhile measure the soup and water into a small saucepan and stir over low heat until blended and almost boiling.
5 Draw the pan off the heat, stir in a little chopped parsley and pour over the eggs. Serve at once.

Sausage and bacon rolls

you will need:

4 streaky bacon rashers	4 oz. (4) chipolata
little tomato ketchup	sausages
	4 soft finger rolls

1 Trim the rind from the bacon and spread each rasher with a little tomato ketchup.
2 Wrap each rasher round a sausage and place under a moderately hot grill. Cook for 10–12 minutes turning frequently.
3 Split the finger rolls, toast the insides and place a sausage and bacon roll in each. Serve warm.

Tuna egg curry

you will need:

2 hard-boiled eggs	½ soup can milk
4 oz. medium noodles	2 level teaspoons curry
½ oz. butter	powder
1 tin undiluted cream of	1 7-oz. tin tuna fish
celery soup	chopped parsley

1 Cut the hard-boiled eggs in quarters.
2 Add the noodles to plenty of boiling salted water, boil gently for 12 minutes, then drain and toss with butter.
3 Meanwhile, measure the soup, milk and curry powder into a saucepan and bring slowly to the boil. Add the hard-boiled egg and flaked tuna fish and heat through very gently until thoroughly hot.
4 Arrange noodles in centre of two warm serving plates and spoon curry mixture on to the centre of each. Sprinkle with chopped parsley and serve.

Toasted sandwiches

As the name implies, these are hot sandwiches, either made with toast or filled and toasted afterwards. They make an ideal snack meal and can be followed with cheese and biscuits or fresh fruit

Devilled pâté sandwiches

you will need:

8 slices of bread
4 oz. liver pâté OR use liver sausage
1 tablespoon finely chopped onion
1 tablespoon tomato ketchup
¼ level teaspoon dry mustard
½ teaspoon Worcestershire sauce
salt and pepper
4 rashers bacon

to garnish:
lettuce

1 Lightly toast the bread on one side only.
2 Pound the liver pâté, onion and seasoning together and spread over the toasted sides of 4 slices.
3 Top each with grilled half slices of bacon and then with remaining bread slices, toasted one side only, and toasted side down. Toast both remaining sides, garnish with crisp lettuce and serve at once.

Egg and mushroom specials

you will need:

8 slices bread
4 hard-boiled eggs
2–4 oz. lightly fried mushrooms
2 tablespoons mayonnaise
salt and pepper
4 rashers bacon

1 Very lightly toast the bread on one side. Finely chop the eggs and mushrooms and blend with the mayonnaise. Season to taste.
2 Warm the mixture and spread over 4 of the toasted slices of bread, and top with remaining bread, toasted side down.
3 Toast both sides of the sandwich, and then top with halved bacon rashers – continue toasting until the bacon is crisp.
4 Serve at once with salad.

Cheese scrambled eggs

you will need:

4 eggs
3 tablespoons milk
3 oz. finely grated Cheddar cheese
salt and pepper
¼ teaspoon made mustard
½ oz. butter
2 slices hot buttered toast

1 Crack the eggs into a basin and add the milk, cheese, salt, pepper and mustard. Whisk lightly with a fork to blend thoroughly.
2 Melt the butter in a small saucepan and add the egg mixture all at once.
3 Stir over gentle heat until the egg begins to thicken. When scrambled but still moist draw the pan off the heat.
4 Spoon on to hot buttered toast and serve with grilled bacon rashers and sautéed mushrooms.

Oven-baked hot dogs

you will need:

6 thin slices bread
2 oz. butter OR margarine
6 back bacon rashers
French mustard
6 frankfurter sausages

1 Trim the crusts from each slice of bread and roll out with a rolling pin to make slices thinner.
2 Spread one side with butter or margarine and place a trimmed bacon rasher on each.
3 Spread with mustard, place a frankfurter in the centre of each and roll up in the bread. Secure with a wooden cocktail stick and pack the rolls close together on a baking sheet, or in a small roasting tin. Brush tops with any leftover butter or margarine, melted.
4 Place above centre of a hot oven (400°F. – Gas Mark 6) and bake for 20–30 minutes until crisp and golden brown.
Note: These can be prepared ahead and baked just when ready to serve.

Fried bread with savoury toppings

you will need:

4 slices bread
2 oz. butter OR margarine

Remove the crusts from the slices of bread and fry in the hot butter or margarine until golden brown on both sides. Top with any of the following and serve at once.

Sardine and cheese – mash the contents of 1 tin sardines (drain oil from the fish and remove the tails), and add ½ teaspoon Worcestershire sauce and a seasoning of salt and pepper. Spread thinly on fried bread. Top with thinly sliced tomato and place under the moderately hot grill for 2–3 minutes. Place a thin slice of cheese on top and return this to the grill until the cheese has melted.

Apple and cheese – peel two small sweet apples and mix with 3 oz. grated Cheddar cheese. Spread over the fried bread and place under a moderately hot grill for 2–3 minutes until cheese has melted and the apple is soft.

Bacon and cheese – trim the rind away from the eight rashers of bacon and grill rashers. Place two cooked rashers on each slice of fried bread, top with a cheese slice and place under moderately hot grill until the cheese has melted.

Barbecue bean sandwiches

you will need:

8 slices bread	4 oz. streaky bacon
1 8-oz. tin beans in	rashers
tomato sauce	4 oz. Cheddar cheese,
1 tablespoon horse-	grated
radish sauce	4 tomato wedges
1 teaspoon made	
mustard	

1 Toast the bread one side only.
2 Heat in a saucepan the beans, horseradish sauce, mustard and bacon, cooked until crisp, then crumbled. Top 4 of the slices on the toasted sides.
3 Top with remaining bread slices, toasted side down. Gently toast top side, top with the grated cheese and toast cheese until it is melting and golden brown.
4 Top with tomato wedges and serve at once.

Devilled roe savoury

you will need:

4 oz. fresh (or 3-oz.	squeeze lemon juice
packet frozen)	2 slices bread
herring roes	butter
1 level tablespoon flour	
1 level teaspoon curry	**to garnish:**
powder	parsley
salt and pepper	wedges of lemon
1 oz. butter	
dash Worcestershire	
sauce	

1 Thaw herring roes if using frozen, and separate.
2 Sift together the flour, curry powder and seasoning.
3 Toss the roes in this and then fry very gently in the melted butter – only a few minutes each side.
4 Add a dash of Worcestershire sauce and the lemon juice to the pan. Cook a further minute, shaking the pan to flavour the roes.
5 Meanwhile toast bread and butter it.
6 Serve the roes on toast and garnish with a sprig of parsley and wedges of lemon.

Creamed haddock with poached egg

you will need:

8 oz. smoked haddock	squeeze lemon juice
fillet	2 eggs
½ pint milk	2 slices bread
1 oz. butter OR	butter
margarine	
1 level tablespoon flour	**to garnish:**
salt and pepper	chopped parsley

1 Cut up the fish and place in a saucepan with the milk. Poach gently for 10–15 minutes. Strain, reserving milk for the sauce, and flake the fish flesh, removing any skin and bone.
2 Melt the butter or margarine in a small saucepan over moderate heat. Stir in the flour and gradually beat in the milk all the time to get a smooth sauce. Cook gently for 2–3 minutes.
3 Season and add lemon juice and flaked fish.
4 Poach the eggs in simmering salted water.
5 Meanwhile toast the bread and butter it.
6 Spoon creamed haddock on to the toast and top with a poached egg. Sprinkle with chopped parsley and serve with grilled tomatoes.

Creamed chicken and egg

you will need:

½ oz. butter OR	2 hard-boiled eggs, cut
margarine	in quarters
2 oz. mushrooms,	1 teaspoon chopped
sliced	parsley
½ tin condensed cream	2 slices bread
of chicken soup	butter

1 Melt the ½ oz. butter or margarine and sauté the mushrooms for 1–2 minutes.
2 Draw the pan off the heat and stir in the soup. Add the eggs and parsley and allow to heat through gently.
3 Meanwhile make the toast and butter it.
4 Spoon mixture on to toast; serve with grilled tomatoes.

Devilled kidneys

you will need:

4 lamb's kidneys	salt and pepper
1 oz. butter	cayenne pepper
¼ pint single cream	mustard
2 level teaspoons flour	2 slices bread
2 teaspoons Worcester-	butter
shire sauce	
1 teaspoon mushroom	**to garnish:**
ketchup	watercress
1 tablespoon sherry	

1 Remove fat round the kidneys, slice kidneys in halves and snip away any core.
2 Add kidneys to the hot butter and fry quickly for 3–4 minutes to brown, reduce heat and cook slowly for further 3–4 minutes.
3 In a basin whisk together the cream, flour, Worcestershire sauce, mushroom ketchup, sherry and seasoning; add to the kidneys, stir to blend, and bring to the boil.
4 Meanwhile toast bread and butter it.
5 Serve the kidneys on the toast garnished with watercress.

Smothered mushrooms

you will need:

2 oz. butter	juice ½ lemon
4–6 oz. small button mushrooms	chopped parsley
	2 slices bread
salt and pepper	butter

1 Melt half the butter in a frying pan and when bubbling add the sliced mushrooms.
2 Season and cook quickly for 2–3 minutes. Shake the pan occasionally or stir to prevent over-browning.
3 Add remaining butter, lemon juice and parsley. Cover and cook gently for a further 5 minutes.
4 Meanwhile toast the bread and butter it.
5 Spoon mushrooms and juice from pan over toast slices and serve.

Kipper and mushroom omelet

you will need:

1 small kipper	4 eggs
1 oz. butter	1 tablespoon water
2 oz. mushrooms, sliced	salt and pepper

1 Place the kipper in a jug, pour over boiling water to cover and leave for 5 minutes. Then drain and flake the flesh, removing any skin and bones.
2 Meanwhile melt the butter in a small omelet or frying pan and gently sauté the mushrooms for 2–3 minutes. Add to the kipper flesh.
3 In a mixing basin whisk together the eggs, water and seasoning. Pour all at once into the hot butter in the pan. Cook over moderate heat and stir quickly with a fork until the eggs begin to thicken. Then cook without stirring until the underside of the omelet is lightly browned.
4 Add the fish and mushroom mixture and spread over the centre of the omelet.
5 With a palette knife or fish slice loosen the omelet round the sides, fold one half over on to the other and turn out on to a warm serving plate.
6 Cut in half and serve with grilled tomatoes.

Kidneys on toast

you will need:

4 back bacon rashers	chopped parsley
3 lamb's kidneys	2 slices bread
seasoned flour	butter

1 Trim and chop the bacon rashers. Lightly fry and keep hot.
2 Cut the kidneys in halves and snip out the core with scissors. Toss kidneys in seasoned flour and then fry in the hot bacon fat for about 8 minutes.
3 Add a little chopped parsley and the cooked bacon to the pan, and re-heat gently.
4 Toast the bread and butter it.
5 Arrange on a plate, pile mixture on top, and serve with extra grilled bacon rashers or grilled tomatoes.

Quick liver pâté

you will need:

3 oz. butter	salt and pepper
8 oz. lamb's liver, sliced	1 tablespoon brandy

1 Melt 1 oz. butter in a saucepan and add the liver. Brown on both sides, cover and cook gently 5 minutes.
2 Draw the pan off the heat and pass the liver through a mincer, using the coarse blade.
3 Add remaining butter, plenty of seasoning and the brandy.
4 Beat well with a wooden spoon until smooth, then pack into a small dish, cover with melted butter or a lid and store in the refrigerator. Do not keep longer than 3–4 days. It should be served with slices of warm toast, quartered tomatoes and fresh lettuce.

Fish toasts

you will need:

8 oz. smoked haddock or cod fillet	4 slices bread
	butter
¼ pint milk	
½ oz. butter OR margarine	**to garnish:**
	lemon wedges
1½ oz. Cheddar cheese	paprika

1 Place the smoked fillet in a small pan with the milk, cover with a lid and poach gently for 10 minutes.
2 Draw the pan off the heat and remove the fish on to a plate. Reserve 1 tablespoon of the milk in which the fish has been poached.
3 When cooled a little, flake the fish into a basin, removing any skin and bones.
4 Add the butter or margarine, cheese and 1 tablespoon of fish-milk. Mix the ingredients thoroughly with a fork.
5 Toast bread and butter it. Divide fish mixture equally between the four hot slices.
6 Spread evenly and heat gently under the grill – just to warm through. Then cut each slice in two and garnish with a wedge of lemon dipped in paprika for a pretty effect.

Welsh rarebit

you will need:

1 oz. butter OR margarine	1 teaspoon mustard
2 tablespoons milk OR beer	½ teaspoon salt
4 oz. grated Cheddar cheese	4 slices bread
	butter

1 Melt the butter in a small saucepan over a low heat. Add the milk or beer, cheese, mustard and salt and stir until mixture is melted and smooth.
2 Draw the pan off the heat and allow to cool and thicken a little.
3 Toast the bread, butter it, and spread the hot mixture over the four slices.
4 Place under a hot grill and cook until bubbling and golden brown.
5 Trim away crust, cut into fingers and serve at once.

Bacon and mushroom snack

you will need:

4 rashers back bacon	2 slices bread
4 large mushrooms	butter
melted butter OR oil for grilling	2 oz. grated Cheddar cheese
salt and pepper	

1 Trim the rinds from the bacon rashers and arrange in the grill pan. Trim the mushrooms and remove stalks, brush with the melted butter or oil, season and place beside the bacon rashers.
2 Place under a hot grill for 2–3 minutes until both are cooked, turning the bacon rashers once.
3 Meanwhile toast the bread and butter it.
4 Arrange the rashers on the toast, top with the mushrooms and the grated cheese.
5 Grill again until the cheese has melted and serve at once.

Hot-weather dishes

When the weather is hot, appetites are low, so you'll need to make food as light, appetising and full of flavour as possible. For example, I like to ring the changes by serving delicious salads with herb breads in place of starchy potatoes. There is an abundance of salad vegetables available – you can serve green salad with mayonnaise, if accompanying cold meat, or tossed in French dressing when served with a hot main dish. It is a good idea to make up a quantity of French dressing in a screwtop jar (shake well before using) so that it can be stored in the refrigerator for next time.

Salad herb breads

Hot-flavoured breads and rolls make the perfect accompaniment to light summer meals. Rolls can be heated by placing on a baking tray in the centre of a hot oven (400°F. – Gas Mark 6) for 6–8 minutes. Serve at once wrapped in a cloth. **Crescent rolls** are delicious if first brushed with a little melted butter, then sprinkled with grated Parmesan cheese and placed at the top of the oven for 7–8 minutes or until beginning to brown.

Hot herb bread

Cut a Vienna loaf into diagonal slices, leaving the bottom crust whole. Spread both sides of each slice with herb butter (see below). Wrap loaf in aluminium foil and heat through in a moderately hot oven (400°F. – Gas Mark 6) for 15–20 minutes. Serve at once in a napkin or leave wrapped in foil to keep warm.

Herb butter

Cream together 2 oz. butter, squeeze of lemon juice and 1 tablespoon finely chopped parsley until soft. Add a pinch of mixed herbs and use as required. Makes enough for 1 loaf.

Garlic butter

Cream together 2 oz. butter with 1 tablespoon finely chopped parsley and a little chopped garlic from a clove which has first been crushed with a little salt. Use as required – makes enough for 1 loaf.

Old-fashioned spiced pork

you will need:

12 oz. pork fillet	¼ level teaspoon salt
¼ level teaspoon ground ginger	
¼ level teaspoon ground cinnamon	**for the stock:**
	1 pork bone, chopped in two
1 level teaspoon paprika	1 large onion, sliced
6 crushed black peppercorns	1 bay leaf
	½ pint water

1 To make the stock, place bone in a saucepan with the onion, bay leaf and water. Bring to the

boil, cover and simmer gently for 30 minutes.

2 Meanwhile cut the pork meat into fairly small pieces and mix with the spices, paprika, peppercorns and salt.

3 Strain the stock and return to the saucepan.

4 Add the meat and spices and bring to the boil, cover and simmer gently until the meat is tender (about 1½–2 hours).

5 Turn into a 1½–2 pint pudding basin and when cool place a plate over the top. Add a few weights and leave until quite cold and set firm. Serve sliced, with mustard, pickles or plum sauce and tossed green salad.

Sausage and egg pie

you will need:

6 oz. short crust pastry	**for the filling:**
milk	3 chipolata sausages
	3 eggs
	salt and pepper

1 Prepare the pastry and divide in half. Roll out one piece to a circle, large enough to line a 7-inch sponge tin. Cover base and sides.

2 Over this arrange the sausages, cartwheel fashion – leaving three spaces for the eggs. Crack these one at a time into each space, and season well with salt and pepper.

3 Roll out the remainder of the pastry and cover the pie. Seal the edges well and roll the pin over the top to cut off excess pastry. Make a small hole in the centre and brush the pie top with a little milk.

4 Place the pie in the centre of a hot oven (400°F. – Gas Mark 6) and bake for 10 minutes. Then lower the heat to moderate (355°F. – Gas Mark 4) and bake for a further 30 minutes.

5 Serve cut in wedges with salad.

Raised pork pie

you will need:

8 oz. seasoned pork sausage meat	**for the pastry:**
	4 oz. plain flour
pinch powdered sage (optional)	½ level teaspoon salt
	1½ oz. white fat or lard
1 hard-boiled egg	2 tablespoons water
	milk for brushing

1 To prepare the filling, add the sage, if required, to the sausage meat and, with lightly floured fingers, shape the meat round the hard-boiled egg. Set aside while preparing the pastry.

2 Sieve the flour and salt into a warm basin.

3 Measure the fat and water into a small saucepan and bring to the boil. Pour immediately on to centre of the sieved flour and mix to a smooth dough with the wooden spoon.

4 Turn out on to a board and knead until smooth.

5 Reserving a little for decoration and for the lid, shape the remainder into a round. Flatten out the centre to make the base, and pinch the edge of the pastry up to make the sides, using thumb and forefinger.

6 Place the sausage meat in the centre. Roll the reserved pieces out to form a lid. Dampen the edge of the pie with a little milk, and place the lid over the top.

7 Pinch the edges to seal and snip round with a pair of scissors. Flute the edge of the pie to make a turret border. Make a hole in the centre and decorate with leaves made from any remaining pastry.

8 Brush with milk and fix a greased band of paper round the pie.

9 Place in the centre of a very hot oven (425°F. – Gas Mark 7) and bake for 20 minutes, then lower the heat to moderate (355°F. – Gas Mark 4) for a further 40 minutes. After 30 minutes remove the band of paper and brush the whole of the pie with extra milk.

10 Serve the pie cold with sliced tomatoes and tossed green salad.

Cheese and tomato flans

you will need:

6 oz. cheese pastry – see recipe, page 4	1 egg
	¼ pint milk
	seasoning
for the filling:	chopped parsley for garnish
3 tomatoes	
2 oz. grated Cheddar cheese	

1 On a lightly floured working surface, roll the pastry out thinly. Using a saucer as a guide, cut out 2 large rounds of pastry and for each fit into two greased individual flan tins.

2 Fit the pastry in without stretching it and prick the base of each with the prongs of the fork.

3 Fill the centre with a piece of crumpled kitchen foil and bake just above centre of a hot oven (400°F. – Gas Mark 6) for 6–8 minutes, until lightly browned and baked.

4 Reserving one tomato for decoration, plunge the others into boiling water for 1 minute. Drain and remove the skins, seeds and chop the flesh coarsely.

5 Arrange the tomato flesh and grated cheese over the base of each flan.

6 Beat together the egg and milk and season well with salt and pepper. Pour into the pie, filling each one to the brim.

7 Return to the oven, this time bake in the centre of a moderate oven (355°F. – Gas Mark 4) for 20 minutes, or until the filling has set. Garnish with the remaining tomato, sliced, and a little chopped parsley.

Home-pressed tongue

you will need:

2 lamb's tongues	¾ pint stock OR water plus stock cube

1 Wash the tongues and place in a deep saucepan. Add the stock and bring to the boil.
2 Cover and simmer 1½–2 hours, or until tender (test the tip of the tongue with a skewer).
3 While still hot peel off the skin and remove any gristle from the base of the tongue.
4 Curling the tongues round, press them into a small mould or basin about 3–4 inches diameter. Place the tongues facing in opposite directions so that they will fit in neatly and tightly.
5 Cover with a sheet of kitchen foil or greased paper and top with a heavy weight. Leave overnight. Serve sliced with cucumber in sour cream (below).

Sausage rolls

you will need:

4 oz. flaky pastry	salt and pepper
6 oz. pork or beef sausage meat	

1 Prepare the pastry as in the basic recipe using half the quantity of ingredients. On a floured board, roll the pastry out thinly to approximately 12 inches × 6 inches. Trim the edges and cut in half lengthwise. Leave to rest.
2 Season the sausage meat and divide into two portions. Using lightly floured hands, roll each portion out to a long 'rope' the length of the pastry strips.
3 Place one down the centre of each strip of pastry. Dampen one edge of the pastry and fold this over the sausage meat to join with the opposite edge. Seal edges well together.
4 With a sharp knife cut each roll into four or six sausage rolls. Place on a wetted baking sheet and make one or two diagonal slashes on top of each. Brush with a little milk or beaten egg and milk.
5 Place above centre in a very hot oven (425°F. – Gas Mark 7) and bake for 20 minutes.
6 Serve warm with a tossed salad.
Makes 8 sausage rolls.

Cucumber in sour cream

Pare and thinly slice ½ cucumber, sprinkle with salt, pepper and a little finely chopped chives. Add 2–3 tablespoons soured cream, a squeeze of lemon juice and chill until ready to serve.

Ham and pork pasties

you will need:

8 oz. prepared puff pastry	little mustard little milk
1 7-oz. tin chopped ham with pork	

1 On a lightly floured working surface, roll the pastry out thinly and using a floured 3–3½ inch round cutter, stamp out 8 rounds. Place 4 of these on a wetted baking tray.
2 Slice the chopped ham with pork into 4 and spread each one with a little mustard. Place on top of pastry circles.
3 Damp edges of the pastry with water and cover with remaining circles. Press gently round the edges to seal and cut a small slit in the centre of each.
4 Brush with a little milk and place fairly high up in a very hot oven (425°F. – Gas Mark 7) and bake for 10 minutes. Then lower the heat to moderate hot (380°F. – Gas Mark 5) and bake for a further 5–10 minutes or until golden brown and crisp.
5 Remove from the oven, allow to cool. Serve with fresh tomato salad.

Pork pasties

you will need:

8 oz. plain short crust pastry	pinch of thyme salt and pepper 2 hard-boiled eggs

for the filling:
8 oz. sausage meat

1 Divide the pastry into 4 portions. Roll each one out to a circle about 5–6 inches across – trim round the plate. Mix sausage meat with thyme and seasoning.
2 Place a portion of sausage meat in the centre of each pastry circle; sprinkle with thyme and top with half a hard-boiled egg, rounded side upward. Damp the rim of the pastry, bring the edges together in the centre and press together gently to seal.
3 Flute the edges by pinching with the thumb and first two fingers.
4 Place on a greased baking tray and glaze with a little beaten egg and milk. Place just above centre of a hot oven (400°F. – Gas Mark 6) and bake for 10 minutes. Then lower the heat to moderate (380°F. – Gas Mark 5) and bake for a further 15–20 minutes. Serve hot or cold with tossed salad.

Cornish pasties

you will need:

4 oz. plain short crust pastry	pinch mixed herbs
	1 tablespoon chopped parsley
for the filling:	salt and pepper
3–4 oz. lean steak	about 1 tablespoon stock or water
1 medium potato, peeled and diced	
1 small onion, skinned and chopped	egg or milk to glaze

1 Trim away fat or gristle from the meat and shred or mince the meat. Mix with the potato, onion, herbs and chopped parsley. Season well with salt and pepper and moisten with a little stock.
2 Divide the pastry into two portions and roll each piece into a circle about 5 inches in diameter. Place half the filling in the centre of each piece and damp the edges.
3 Bring the edges of the pastry up together in the centre over the filling, and press gently together all round to seal. Flute the join by pinching between the thumb and first two fingers.
4 Place the pasties on a greased baking sheet, glaze with a little beaten egg and milk or milk and bake in the centre of a hot oven (400°F. – Gas Mark 6) for the first 10 minutes then reduce to fairly hot (375°F. – Gas Mark 5) for a further 15–20 minutes. Serve cold with lettuce and cucumber salad.

Potato and herring salad

you will need:

1 lb. boiled potatoes	1 carton soured cream
3–4 marinated or pickled herring fillets	1 tablespoon lemon juice
1 small green pepper, seeded and finely chopped	$\frac{1}{2}$ level teaspoon paprika
1 tablespoon finely chopped parsley OR chives	salt and pepper
	1 lettuce

1 Cut the cooled potatoes into neat dice and the herrings into small pieces (soak herring in milk first if salty).
2 Add the pepper, parsley or chives, sour cream, lemon juice and seasonings to taste.
3 Heap the salad in lettuce cups arranged in pairs, and serve with buttered brown bread slices or sliced cooked bacon or ham.

Soused herrings

you will need:

4 herrings, with heads removed	$\frac{1}{4}$ pint water
4 tablespoons malt vinegar	few peppercorns
	1 bay leaf

1 Wash the herrings under cold water and scrape away any loose scales with a knife. Trim off the fins with scissors and cut off the tails.
2 Slit the herrings lengthways and remove the roes.
3 Place each herring cut side down on a working surface and press sharply down the backbone to loosen it. Turn fish over, carefully pull away any bone and split into fillets.
4 Roll up the fillets and pack closely together in a 1–1½-pint pie dish.
5 Mix the vinegar and water and pour over the herrings. Add the peppercorns and bay leaf.
6 Cover with a greased paper or a lid, place in the centre of a very moderate oven (355°F. – Gas Mark 4) and bake for 40–45 minutes.
7 Allow cooked herrings to cool in the liquid, then drain and serve with potato salad, crisp fresh lettuce and tomato halves.

Variation

With trout – follow the recipe above using 4 small trout in place of the herrings. Bone them in the same manner as the herrings.

Shellfish cocktail

you will need:

6 oz. prepared prawns	2 tablespoons thick cream
2–3 crisp washed lettuce leaves	dash Tabasco sauce
	1 teaspoon Worcestershire sauce
for the cocktail sauce:	
2 tablespoons mayonnaise	squeeze lemon juice
2 tablespoons tomato ketchup	**to decorate:**
	lemon wedges

1 Prepare the shellfish and set aside in a basin. Shred the lettuce leaves finely and put into the base of two glasses. Set aside while mixing the sauce.
2 In a basin combine together the mayonnaise, ketchup and cream. Stir in the Tabasco sauce, Worcestershire sauce and lemon juice to taste.
3 Add the prepared shellfish to the sauce and spoon into the glasses over the lettuce base. Chill until ready to serve.
4 Serve with lemon and buttered brown bread.

Variation

Lobster or crab cocktail – follow the recipe given above, using 1 (7-oz.) tin lobster or crab meat, drained and flaked.

Fish mayonnaise

you will need:

6–8 oz. cooked white fish – turbot, cod OR halibut	1 tablespoon grated onion
1 tablespoon cream OR top of the milk	salt and pepper
	crisp lettuce leaves
3 tablespoons mayonnaise	tomato slices

1 Flake the fish, removing any skin and bones.
2 Blend the mayonnaise with cream or top of the

milk and grated onion. Fold the fish into the mayonnaise, season and chill.

3 Spoon the fish salad on to crisp washed lettuce leaves and arrange on a serving platter with sliced tomato. Serve with buttered brown bread.

Variation

Chicken mayonnaise – follow the recipe given above, using cooked shredded chicken instead of white fish.

Devilled egg and ham salad

you will need:

3 hard-boiled eggs
1 tablespoon mayonnaise
salt and pepper
¼ teaspoon made mustard
½ small onion, grated
pinch curry powder
4 oz. sliced cooked ham or bacon

to garnish:
cress

1 Slice the eggs in halves lengthwise. Remove the yolks with a teaspoon, put in a small basin and reserve the whites.
2 Mash the yolks with a fork and blend in the mayonnaise. Season well and add the mustard, onion and curry powder.
3 Refill the whites with heaped teaspoons of the mixture. Arrange on a serving platter with the slices of ham rolled neatly.
4 Garnish the egg with a little cress and serve the platter with a tossed green salad and buttered brown bread.

Iced prawn curry

you will need:

6 oz. prepared prawns

for the sauce:
½ small onion, finely chopped
1 oz. butter
1 level teaspoon flour
2 level tablespoons curry powder
1 8-oz. tin tomatoes
½ level teaspoon salt
1 level teaspoon sugar
1 tablespoon sweet mango chutney
¼ pint mayonnaise
Tabasco sauce
2 tablespoons single cream
juice ½ lemon

6 oz. long grain rice
¼ level teaspoon pepper
¼ level teaspoon salt
¼ level teaspoon dry mustard
1 tablespoon vinegar
3 tablespoons salad oil

to garnish:
chopped parsley

1 Prepare the prawns then set aside while making the sauce.
2 Sauté the onion gently in the butter until soft. Stir in the flour and curry powder, then add the tomatoes plus liquid from tin, salt, sugar and chutney.
3 Bring to the boil, stirring well; cover and simmer for 30 minutes.
4 Draw the pan off the heat and sieve the curry sauce into a basin.
5 Add the mayonnaise, Tabasco sauce, cream and lemon juice. Stir in prepared prawns and chill until ready to serve.
6 Cook the rice in plenty of boiling salted water for 8 minutes, then drain, wash in cold water to cool and drain again. Turn into a basin. Into a small screwtop jar measure the salt, pepper, mustard, vinegar and oil for the dressing. Cover and shake well to mix. Pour over the cooked rice, toss well and chill until ready to serve.
7 Spoon the rice on to a serving platter and make a well in the middle. Pour in the prawn curry, sprinkle with chopped parsley and serve with buttered brown bread.

Poached fish cutlets in mayonnaise

you will need:

2 small cod or halibut steaks
½ lemon, sliced
1 bay leaf
½ level teaspoon salt
2 tablespoons mayonnaise
1 tablespoon cream OR top of the milk
1 level teaspoon aspic jelly crystals
1 tablespoon hot water

to decorate:
cucumber slices
chopped parsley

1 Rinse the cutlets and snip away the fins. Place in a saucepan and just cover with cold water; add the lemon, bay leaf and salt. Bring slowly to the boil, cover and poach, allowing 3–4 minutes for cod, 10–15 minutes for halibut. Allow to cool in the liquid.
2 Drain the fish from the liquid and carefully lift away any skin and bone. Arrange on a rack or wire cooling tray and set over a plate.
3 Combine the mayonnaise, cream and aspic jelly dissolved in the hot water. Stir until beginning to set (set basin in iced water to speed up), then spoon quickly over the fish.
4 Chill for at least 1 hour to set firm, garnish with cucumber slices and chopped parsley and serve with tossed green salad and buttered brown bread.

Trout with bacon

you will need:

2 trout
seasoned flour
1 oz. butter
4 bacon rashers
chopped parsley

1 Have the trout cleaned and, if liked, heads removed.
2 Roll in seasoned flour and add to the hot butter in a frying pan.
3 Fry gently for 3–4 minutes on each side. After turning the fish, add the trimmed bacon rashers.

4 Sprinkle with chopped parsley and serve with the hot butter and juices from the pan.

Prawn and cottage cheese cocottes

you will need:

2 small eggs	1 teaspoon made
3 tablespoons hot milk	mustard
1 rounded tablespoon	salt and pepper
fresh white bread-	squeeze lemon juice
crumbs	
4 oz. prepared prawns	**to garnish:**
1 8-oz. carton cottage	chopped parsley
cheese	

1 Lightly mix the eggs and milk and pour over the breadcrumbs in a small basin.
2 Stir in the remaining ingredients, season well and add lemon juice to taste.
3 Spoon the mixture into one greased one pint baking dish. Stand in a shallow baking or roasting tin with water 1 inch up the sides.
4 Bake in moderately hot oven (375°F. – Gas Mark 5) until set about 45 minutes.
5 Sprinkle with chopped parsley and serve with a tossed salad.

Jambalaya

you will need:

1 small onion, finely	pinch pepper
chopped	1 bay leaf
3 tablespoons cooking	8 oz. prepared prawns
oil	OR scampi
1 lb. tomatoes	4 oz. cooked ham, cut
1 green pepper, seeded	in one slice
and shredded	
6 oz. long grain rice	**to decorate:**
½ pint boiling water	chopped parsley
1 level teaspoon salt	

1 Sauté the onion gently in the hot oil to soften (about 5 minutes). Meanwhile plunge the tomatoes into boiling water for 1 minute, drain and peel off the skins. Cut in half, remove the seeds and chop tomato flesh.
2 Add tomato, green pepper and rice to the onion. Sauté gently for a further 5 minutes, stirring occasionally, then stir in the boiling water, seasoning and bay leaf.
3 Cover with a tight-fitting lid and simmer gently, stirring occasionally, until the rice is tender and the liquid absorbed (about 30 minutes). Add a little extra liquid if required.
4 Draw the pan off the heat, remove the bay leaf and add prawns or scampi and the diced ham.
5 Spoon the mixture into a casserole. Cover and place in a moderately hot oven (350°F. – Gas Mark 5) and allow to heat through for 5–10 minutes. Sprinkle with chopped parsley, serve with crusty bread and butter and tossed salad.

Baked chicory and ham

you will need:

4 medium heads of	2 oz. grated Parmesan
chicory	cheese
salt	pinch pepper
½ pint milk	4 thin slices of cooked
2 eggs	ham

1 Trim the outside leaves from the chicory and put heads in a saucepan and just cover with cold water. Bring up to the boil, then drain the chicory, return to the saucepan and re-cover with cold water.
2 Add a pinch salt, cover with a lid and simmer gently for about 30 minutes or until tender.
3 Meanwhile heat the milk gently, then pour on to the lightly beaten eggs whisking all the time. Strain back into the milk saucepan.
4 Stir over very gentle heat until just thick enough to coat the back of a spoon – do not allow the mixture to boil.
5 Draw the pan off the heat and stir in half the cheese and a good seasoning of salt and pepper.
6 Drain the cooked chicory, wrap each head in a slice of ham and place in a buttered fireproof dish. Pour the cheese custard over the chicory; sprinkle with remaining cheese and grill until brown.

Rice curry salad with ham

you will need:

6 oz. long grain rice	¼ level teaspoon salt
1 small packet frozen	1 level teaspoon curry
peas, thawed	powder
1 green pepper, seeded	1 tablespoon vinegar
and chopped	2 tablespoons salad oil
4 oz. prepared prawns	4 oz. cooked, sliced
2 tablespoons chutney	ham

1 Sprinkle the rice in a pan of boiling salted water and cook rapidly for 10 minutes. Drain and rinse with cold water to cool, drain again then spoon into a large basin.
2 Add the peas, cooked according to instructions on packet, chopped pepper, prawns, chutney, salt and curry powder.
3 Blend the vinegar and oil and add to the ingredients. Toss and mix thoroughly.
4 Serve the salad with the sliced ham and a few extra crisp washed lettuce leaves.

Grilled salmon cutlets

you will need:

2 salmon cutlets	**to garnish:**
salt and pepper	lemon slices
melted butter	

1 Wipe the cutlets (if frozen allow to thaw out) and season. *continued*

2 Brush with a little melted butter and place in the base of the grill pan, at least 3 inches from the heat. Grill under moderate heat for 5 minutes, then turn. Brush second side with melted butter and grill for a further 5 minutes.
3 Test by pressing near the centre bone – flesh should flake easily.
4 Lift on to a warm serving platter, pour over butter from grill pan. Garnish with lemon slices, and serve with green peas and buttered potatoes.

Halibut with lemon egg sauce

you will need:

2 tablespoons oil	¼ pint milk
2 small onions, sliced	salt and pepper
2 halibut steaks	1 tablespoon lemon
salt and pepper	juice
	1 egg yolk

for the sauce:
½ oz. butter OR
  margarine
1 level tablespoon flour

to decorate:
chopped parsley

1 Heat the oil in a saucepan and add the onions. Fry gently until just coloured. Add the halibut steaks and season them. Pour in sufficient water to barely cover the fish. Cover the pan and bring slowly to the boil.
2 Lower the heat and poach gently for 25–30 minutes.
3 Meanwhile to prepare the sauce melt the butter or margarine in a small saucepan and stir in the flour. Cook gently over medium heat for 1–2 minutes but do not brown. Stir in the milk gradually, beating well to get a really smooth sauce.
4 Bring to the boil, lower the heat and cook gently for about 2 minutes. Season well, draw the pan off the heat and add the lemon juice and stir in the yolk.
5 Remove the fish from the pan and arrange on a serving platter, pour over the sauce, sprinkle with finely chopped parsley and serve with green peas and sauté potatoes.

Oven chicken barbecue

you will need:

2 tablespoons cooking oil	1 onion, sliced
2 chicken joints	1 tablespoon Worcestershire sauce
for the barbecue baste:	2 tablespoons tomato ketchup
¼ pint tomato juice	1 teaspoon made mustard
2 tablespoons vinegar	salt and pepper
1 teaspoon sugar	

1 Heat the oil and quickly brown the chicken joints on both sides. Lift from the pan and place joints in a small baking or roasting tin.

2 In a saucepan, combine together the tomato juice, vinegar, sugar, onion, Worcestershire sauce, ketchup, mustard and a good seasoning of salt and pepper. Bring up to the boil and pour over the chicken joints.
3 Place the chicken in the centre of a moderate oven (355°F. – Gas Mark 4) and bake for 1 hour, basting every 15 minutes with the barbecue baste. Serve with tossed salad.

Sautéed chicken

you will need:

2 chicken joints	2 tablespoons finely chopped onion
flour for coating	juice ½ lemon
1–2 oz. butter for frying	½ level teaspoon salt
	pinch pepper
for the marinade:	pinch dried thyme
4 tablespoons oil	

1 Wipe the chicken joints and trim neatly. Place in a shallow dish and set aside while preparing the marinade.
2 Combine the oil, onion, lemon juice, seasoning and herbs. Mix well and pour over the chicken. Leave to marinate 1 hour, turning joints occasionally.
3 Lift the joints from the marinade, allow any excess to drain away and coat the joints with flour.
4 Heat the butter in a frying pan and add the chicken joints skin-side up. Brown on both sides over high heat, then lower the heat and cook gently for 30–35 minutes, turning occasionally to brown evenly.
5 Serve the joints topped with soured cream and snipped chives, and accompanied by jacket potatoes, tossed tomato and lettuce salad.

Fried chicken with lemon rice

you will need:

2 chicken joints	**for the lemon rice:**
1 rounded tablespoon flour	6 oz. long grain rice
1 level teaspoon salt	1 level teaspoon salt
1 level dessertspoon curry powder	½ pint water
2 oz. butter for frying	finely grated rind ½ lemon
1 banana, peeled and sliced	½ oz. butter
	to garnish:
	lemon slices

1 Wipe the chicken joints and trim away any loose skin.
2 Sift the flour, salt and curry powder on to a plate and dip the joints both sides to coat thoroughly.
3 Heat the butter in a frying pan and add the chicken, skin side down. Fry over fairly high heat to brown both sides, then lower the heat and cook gently 25–30 minutes or until tender. Turn occasionally to cook evenly.

4 Meanwhile measure the rice, salt, water and grated lemon rind into a saucepan. Bring to the boil, stir once, then cover, lower the heat and cook gently 15–20 minutes, or until the water is absorbed and rice quite tender. Add butter and fork up the rice.

5 Lift the chicken joints from the pan on to a warm serving platter. Add the sliced banana to the hot butter and fry gently for about 2–3 minutes, then spoon over the chicken joints and serve with the lemon rice. Garnish with lemon slices.

Pork chops with barbecue baste

you will need:

2 large pork chops	2 tablespoons vinegar
salt	2 dessertspoons mango chutney
for the barbecue baste:	1 teaspoon fresh mustard
1 oz. butter OR margarine	1 level teaspoon castor sugar
1 small onion, finely chopped	1 tablespoon Worcestershire sauce
2 tablespoons tomato ketchup	

1 Trim away any rind from the pork chops, sprinkle with salt and place in a small baking or roasting tin. Set aside while preparing baste.

2 Melt the butter or margarine in a small saucepan, add the onion and sauté until tender (about 5 minutes).

3 Mix the remaining ingredients and add to the onion in the saucepan. Bring to the boil, stirring well, and then draw the pan off the heat.

4 Place the pork chops in the centre of a hot oven (400°F. – Gas Mark 6) and cook 15 minutes. Remove from the heat, pour away any fat in the pan and pour the barbecue sauce over the chops.

5 Reduce oven heat to moderate (355°F. – Gas Mark 4) and continue cooking for a further 30 minutes, basting occasionally.

6 Serve the chops with the baste spooned over. Accompany with creamy mashed potato and green peas.

Ratatouille

you will need:

2–3 tablespoons corn oil	2–3 courgettes, peeled and sliced
1 onion, peeled and sliced	8 oz. tomatoes
1 green pepper, deseeded and shredded	2 oz. grated Cheddar cheese or little chopped parsley, for serving
1 aubergine, skinned and cut in cubes	

1 Heat the oil in a large saucepan and fry the onion and pepper gently for 5 minutes until soft, covered with a lid.

2 Add the aubergine and courgettes, recover and simmer gently for a further 30 minutes.

3 Plunge the tomatoes into boiling water for 1 minute. Drain and peel away the skins. Cut into quarters and remove the seeds. Add the tomato flesh to the saucepan and cook for a further 15 minutes. Then sprinkle with cheese or parsley.

4 Serve with grilled chops or steak.

Scotch mushrooms

you will need:

4 small open mushrooms	brown breadcrumbs for coating
oil and vinegar dressing	cooking oil for shallow frying
6 oz. sausage meat	
lightly beaten egg	

1 Wash and peel the mushrooms and remove the stalks. Place in a shallow dish and spoon over the dressing. Leave to marinate for 1 hour.

2 Put sausage meat on a clean working surface and divide into 4 portions. With lightly floured hands, enclose each mushroom in sausage meat. Shape into a neat round, making sure the mushroom is completely covered.

3 Dip each patty first into beaten egg, then in breadcrumbs, coating on both sides and patting on crumbs firmly.

4 Fry in hot shallow oil for 8–10 minutes, turning until golden brown on both sides. Drain and serve cold, sliced in halves, with a hard-boiled egg, lettuce and tomato salad.

Lamb chops with lemon butter

you will need:

2 lean lamb chops	2 tablespoons water
1 oz. butter	salt and pepper
grated rind and juice ½ lemon	1 tablespoon chopped parsley

1 Brown the chops over high heat in the hot butter. Then lift out into a casserole dish.

2 Add the lemon rind, juice, water and seasoning to the butter and bring to the boil. Pour over the chops and sprinkle with parsley.

3 Cover the casserole with a lid, place in the centre of a moderate oven (355°F. – Gas Mark 4) and cook 1 hour.

4 Spoon the juice over the chops and serve with sauté potatoes and whole kernel sweet corn.

Salads to serve with cold meats or on their own

Rice salad

Boil 2 oz. long grain rice in boiling, salted water for 8 minutes. Then drain and run under cold water to cool. Spoon into a mixing basin and add 2–3 tablespoons oil and vinegar dressing, 2 oz. finely grated cheese and 3–4 oz. diced cooked meat or luncheon meat, toss and serve.

Green salad

Choose a selection of green salad, such as lettuce, watercress, cucumber, chicory and prepare according to kind. Toss in oil and vinegar dressing and serve with sliced meat.

Russian salad

Cut cooked potato, carrot and turnip into dice and mix with other cooked vegetables such as peas, whole kernel sweet corn and French beans. Add enough mayonnaise to blend all the ingredients together. Serve with cold chicken or ham.

Egg salad

Cut 2 hard-boiled eggs in half lengthwise and scoop out the yolks into a mixing basin. Mash with a fork and add 2 tablespoons mayonnaise and 4 oz. shelled prawns. Heap the mixture back into the egg white halves and serve with crisp washed lettuce leaves.

Cabbage salad

Finely shred half a white cabbage and add grated raw carrot, cheese and apple or chopped nuts. Add enough mayonnaise to bind the ingredients and serve with sliced meat.

Tomato salad

Slice fresh tomatoes and arrange in a shallow dish with sliced onion rings. Pour over 2–3 tablespoons oil and vinegar dressing and allow to marinate 1–2 hours before serving. Serve with poultry or bacon.

Ham salad

Thinly slice and then shred equal quantities cooked ham and Cheddar cheese. Bind with mayonnaise and heap on crisp washed lettuce leaves and serve.

Creamy slaw salad

you will need:

¼ white cabbage, finely shredded	1 8-oz. tin pineapple rings
1 8-oz. carton cottage cheese	1 tablespoon chopped spring onions
3 tablespoons soured cream	salt and pepper

1 Toss the shredded cabbage, cottage cheese and soured cream together.

2 Drain the tin of pineapple rings, and chop fruit coarsely. Add to the salad along with the chopped onion and a seasoning of salt and pepper.

3 Serve with brown bread and butter and sliced cooked ham.

Peach and cottage cheese salad

you will need:

8 oz. cottage cheese	1 8-oz. tin peach slices, drained from the juice
1 tablespoon seedless raisins	
1 oz. coarsely chopped walnuts	
salt and pepper	**to garnish:**
3–4 crisp, washed lettuce leaves	chopped chives or parsley

1 Combine together the cottage cheese, seedless raisins and nuts.

2 Season well with salt and pepper and heap on to a base of lettuce.

3 Top with the peach slices and garnish with chives or parsley.

Waldorf salad

you will need:

3 crisp dessert apples	2–3 stalks celery
1–2 tablespoons mayonnaise	1–2 oz. coarsely chopped walnuts

1 Wipe the apples and leave the skin on if a pretty colour. Quarter, core and cut apples in neat dice.

2 Blend at once with the mayonnaise and add the thinly shredded celery.

3 Chill until ready to serve then, at the last moment, fold in the coarsely chopped walnuts and garnish with the watercress.

4 Serve with sliced ham and tongue.

Rosy salad

you will need:

1 small cooked beetroot	2–3 tablespoons oil and vinegar dressing
2–3 stalks celery	watercress
2 crisp dessert apples	

1 Skin and cut the beetroot into neat small dice. Slice celery stalks thinly and peel, core and cut the apples into small dice.

2 Mix all together with the oil and vinegar dressing until apples and celery take on a pink colour from the beetroot.

3 Pile into a serving dish and surround with sprigs of washed watercress.

4 Serve with sliced corned beef or luncheon meat.

Salmon and cottage cheese salad

you will need:

1 8-oz. carton cottage cheese
1 small tin pink salmon
2-3 tablespoons soured cream
3 tablespoons chopped, deseeded green pepper
1 tablespoon chopped onion
2 tomatoes, sliced seasoning
1-2 tablespoons oil and vinegar dressing

1 Combine together the cottage cheese, the drained and flaked salmon flesh, soured cream, green pepper and onion.
2 Serve over the sliced tomatoes which have been sprinkled with seasoning and tossed in oil and vinegar dressing.

Cottage cheese luncheon salad

you will need:

1 8-oz. tin pineapple rings
1 8-oz. carton cottage cheese
salt and pepper
2-3 oz. coarsely chopped walnuts
1 bunch crisp watercress

1 Drain the pineapple rings from the tin and arrange 2 rings on each salad plate.
2 Top with half the cottage cheese, season with salt and pepper if liked and sprinkle with walnuts.
3 Serve with the washed watercress, sliced brown bread and butter and cooked chicken.

Chocolate and coffee mousse

you will need:

2 oz. plain chocolate
½ oz. butter
1 tablespoon coffee essence
2 eggs
¼ pint double cream

to decorate:
chopped walnuts

1 Break the chocolate into pieces and place in a small basin set over a pan of hot water. Stir until melted and smooth.
2 Add the butter, coffee essence and egg yolks and stir for further 2 minutes.
3 Remove the basin from the heat and fold in the stiffly beaten egg whites and whipped cream.
4 Spoon into two individual serving glasses and chill several hours. Just before serving, top with chopped walnuts.

Ice cream and caramel raisin sauce

you will need:

for the sauce:
4 oz. soft brown sugar
4 tablespoons single cream
1½ oz. butter
1½ oz. seedless raisins, soaked in water
2 scoops ice cream

1 Combine the sugar and cream in a small saucepan, add the butter and stir over low heat until the sugar melts.
2 Bring to the boil and allow to simmer gently for 5 minutes or until the mixture is a caramel colour.
3 Draw the pan off the heat, stir in the raisins and allow to cool. Spoon the ice cream into individual serving glasses and pour over the sauce. Serve with wafers.

Variation
Chocolate and coffee sauce

you will need:

2 rounded tablespoons Demerara sugar
½ teaspoon instant coffee
2 teaspoons water
¼ oz. butter
1 packet chocolate chips OR plain chocolate broken in pieces
2 scoops ice cream

1 Measure the sugar, coffee, water and butter into a small saucepan. Bring slowly to the boil, stirring to dissolve the sugar.
2 Draw the pan off the heat and stir in the chocolate until melted and smooth. Then serve quickly over ice cream.

Home made vanilla ice

you will need:

¼ pint double cream
1½ oz. icing sugar
a few drops vanilla essence
2 egg whites

1 Lightly whip the cream, then whisk in the sifted icing sugar and a few drops of vanilla essence.
2 Whisk the egg whites until stiff and fold into the mixture.
3 Pour into the ice making tray and place in the freezer compartment of the refrigerator. Freeze until firm, whisking the mixture at least once during freezing to get a creamy smooth consistency.

Variation

Coffee ice – add 1 teaspoon coffee essence to the basic recipe. A little grated plain chocolate could also be stirred in.

Baked custard

you will need:

1 egg	few drops vanilla
1 level tablespoon	essence
sugar	grated nutmeg
¼ pint milk	

1 Break the egg into a small basin. Add the sugar and milk and whisk lightly to blend.
2 Add the vanilla essence (if used) and strain the mixture into a buttered ½-pint baking dish.
3 Grate nutmeg (if used) over the surface and place the dish in a larger baking or roasting tin. Add cold water to come halfway up the sides of the dish.
4 Place in the centre of a slow oven (335°F. – Gas Mark 3) and bake for 25–30 minutes or until set firm.
5 Lift the dish from the baking tin and serve warm, or chilled with stewed fruit.

Apple shortcake

you will need:

3 oz. plain flour	2 oz. margarine
3 oz. fine semolina	2 eating apples,
2 oz. castor sugar	washed and dried

1 Sift together the flour and semolina into a basin. Add the sugar and rub in the fat.
2 Press half the mixture over the base of a greased shallow 7-inch-diameter sponge-cake tin.
3 Grate the unpeeled apple over the mixture, then press remainder on top.
4 Place in a moderate oven (355°F. – Gas Mark 4) and bake for 20–30 minutes.
5 Allow to cool for 5 minutes, then cut in wedges and serve with cream.

Variations:

Mincemeat shortcake – follow the recipe above, omitting the grated apple. Instead spread 2 tablespoons mincemeat over the shortcake mixture. Top with the remaining shortcake mixture and bake as directed above.

Raspberry shortcake – follow the recipe above, omitting the shredded apple. Instead arrange 1 small packet thawed frozen raspberries over the shortcake base. Top with second layer and bake as directed above.

With cream – any apple shortcake left over is delicious served cold with ice cream or fresh cream.

Orange compôte

you will need:

3 oranges	4 tablespoons water
4 oz. castor sugar	juice of ½ lemon

1 Place the oranges together in a bowl, cover with boiling water and leave to stand for 5 minutes.
2 Drain, mark the skin in quarters and then peel away the orange skin. Scrape away any white pith still adhering to the orange flesh.
3 Slice the oranges across and place in a serving dish.
4 Measure the sugar and water into a saucepan. Place over low heat and stir until the sugar has dissolved.
5 Bring to the boil, simmer for 1 minute and draw off the heat.
6 Stir in the strained lemon juice, cool for a few moments and then pour over the orange slices. Cool, then chill before serving.

Fruit salad

you will need:

4 oz. castor sugar	1 dessert apple, peeled
¼ pint water	and diced*
1 tablespoon kirsch or	1 banana, peeled and
sweet sherry	sliced*
1 dessert pear, peeled	4 oz. black grapes,
and sliced*	halved and seeded

* Or cherries, halved and stoned; oranges cut into segments; or drained tinned pineapple chunks

1 Prepare a syrup by dissolving the sugar in the water over low heat. Bring to the boil and simmer for 2 minutes, then draw the pan off the heat.
2 Add the kirsch or sherry and put the syrup to cool while preparing the fruit.
3 Add the prepared fruit to the syrup (dip apples and bananas in a little lemon juice to keep white colour). Chill until ready to serve.
4 Serve with cream or ice cream.

Baked fresh apricots

you will need:

1 lb. fresh apricots	juice of 1 lemon
3 oz. castor sugar	

1 Place the washed, whole apricots in a fireproof dish, add the sugar and the strained lemon juice.
2 Cover with a lid and place in the centre of a slow oven (300°F. – Gas Mark 2) and bake for 1 hour.
3 Cool and serve with cream or ice cream.

Fresh orange jelly

you will need:

1 level tablespoon powdered gelatine	½ pint fresh orange juice
2 rounded tablespoons castor sugar	squeeze lemon juice
2 tablespoons water	1 orange

1 Measure the gelatine, sugar and water into a saucepan, and leave to soak for 5 minutes. Place over very gentle heat and stir until the gelatine is dissolved, but do not boil.
2 Draw the pan off the heat and stir in the strained orange and lemon juice.
3 Stir to blend, and then cool until just warm. Pour into a small mould or 2 individual glasses and chill until set firm.
4 Peel the orange leaving it whole, then slice thinly. Arrange the pieces of orange over the top or around the sides of the set jelly (turned out if in mould). Sprinkle with sugar and serve with cream.

Variation

Lemon jelly – follow the recipe above, using ½ pint made up lemon squash. Prepare the squash to taste and omit the lemon juice in the recipe.

Seafoam pudding

you will need:

2 oz. cornflour	4 oz. castor sugar
1 pint water	2 egg whites
finely grated rind and juice of 2 lemons	

1 Measure the cornflour into a saucepan, add the water and grated lemon rind. Stir to blend, then bring to the boil, stirring all the time.
2 Cook for 1–2 minutes until clear, then draw the pan off the heat and stir in the sugar and lemon juice. Set the pan aside for about 5 minutes, until cool enough for the hand to be held comfortably against the sides.
3 Beat the egg whites until stiff, then using a metal spoon fold into the mixture.
4 Pour into a wetted 1½ pint mould or into a serving dish. Leave for several hours until quite cold and set firm. Unmould if necessary; serve with cream.

Warm food for cold days

Cold weather encourages hearty appetites so make your meals nourishing and satisfying and serve them piping hot. Menus at this time of the year tend to be starchy so concentrate on serving plenty of vegetables and as much fresh fruit as you can find.

Sweet corn soup

you will need:

1 11-oz. tin whole kernel sweet corn	1 level teaspoon flour
¾ pint milk	½ level teaspoon salt
½ oz. butter OR margarine	¼ pint single cream
½ small onion, finely chopped	**to garnish:** chopped parsley

1 Empty the sweet corn into a saucepan and add ½ pint of the milk. Simmer for 30 minutes or until tender, then draw the pan off the heat and rub the soup through a sieve to make a purée.
2 Melt the butter or margarine in a saucepan over low heat and add the onion. Cook gently covered with a lid until the onion is tender.
3 Stir in the flour, remaining milk, corn purée and the salt. Bring up to the boil, stirring all the time.
4 Simmer gently for 5 minutes, then draw the pan off the heat and stir in the cream. Serve sprinkled with chopped parsley.

Lentil soup

you will need:

4 oz. lentils	1 onion, peeled and finely chopped
2 pints stock or water	1 level teaspoon flour
¼ oz. butter OR margarine	½ level teaspoon salt

1 Soak the lentils in the water overnight.
2 Next day, melt the fat in a saucepan and add the onion and fry gently for 5 minutes until soft. Stir in the flour and cook for 1 minute.
3 Gradually stir in the soaked lentils stock and the salt. Bring up to the boil, then lower the heat and simmer gently for 1½ hours.
4 When the lentils are quite soft, draw the pan off the heat and rub through a sieve.
5 Return the soup to the saucepan, reheat, check seasoning and serve.

Potato and watercress soup

you will need:

1lb. potatoes	¾ pint hot stock or water
½ oz. margarine	½ level teaspoon salt
1 small onion, peeled and finely chopped	¼ pint milk
1 bunch watercress	

1 Peel and coarsely slice the potatoes. Melt the fat in a saucepan and add the prepared potatoes
continued

and onion. Sauté gently for 5 minutes but do not allow to brown.

2 Wash the watercress thoroughly and remove lower halves of stems. Chop coarsely and add half to the saucepan.

3 Stir in the stock or water and the salt and bring to the boil.

4 Lower the heat and simmer gently for 1 hour. When the potatoes are quite soft, draw the pan off the heat and rub the soup through a sieve.

5 Return the soup to the saucepan with the milk, reheat, check seasoning, stir in reserved watercress and serve.

Scotch broth

you will need:

8 oz. middle neck of mutton	½ swede, diced
1 pint water	2 stalks celery, shredded
½ level teaspoon salt	
1 oz. pearl barley	**to garnish:**
1 onion, finely chopped	1 teaspoon chopped parsley
1 carrot, diced	

1 Wipe the meat and cut away any surplus fat. Remove any meat from the bones and shred it finely.

2 Place the meat and bone in a large saucepan, cover with water and add salt.

3 Place the pearl barley in a small saucepan, cover with water, bring to the boil, strain and add to the soup pot.

4 Bring soup to the boil, skim, cover with a lid and simmer for 1 hour.

5 Add the prepared vegetables except the parsley and simmer for another hour.

6 Remove the bone, check the seasoning, sprinkle with chopped parsley and serve.

Country beef stew

you will need:

12 oz. lean stewing steak	8 oz. carrots, sliced
seasoned flour	¼ pint stock OR water plus stock cube
1 oz. lard OR dripping	salt and pepper
2 medium onions, sliced	

1 Wipe the meat and trim away any fat or gristle. Cut the meat into cubes and roll in seasoned flour.

2 Heat the lard or dripping in a frying pan, add the meat and fry over fairly high heat until the meat is browned on all sides.

3 Transfer the meat to a casserole dish and add the onions and carrots.

4 Add about 1 tablespoon of the seasoned flour to the hot fat in the pan and continue to cook over moderate heat, stirring well, until the flour is a nutty brown colour.

5 Gradually stir in the hot stock and bring to the boil, continuing to stir all the time. Draw the pan off the heat and strain over the contents of the casserole dish. Check seasoning.

6 Cover with a lid, place in the centre of a slow oven (355°F. – Gas Mark 3) and cook for 2½–3 hours, or until the meat is tender.

7 Serve with boiled or creamed potatoes and an extra vegetable if wished.

Mexican mince

you will need:

1 tablespoon olive oil	1 teaspoon Worcestershire sauce
1 onion, chopped	
1 clove of garlic, crushed with a little salt	1 8-oz. tin baked beans in tomato sauce
8 oz. minced beef	¼ pint stock OR vegetable cooking water
1 level tablespoon flour	
1 8-oz. tin tomatoes	

1 Heat the oil in a saucepan and gently fry the onion and garlic until soft.

2 Brown the meat, sprinkle in the flour, stir to mix and add the tomatoes, plus liquid from the tin, Worcestershire sauce, beans and stock.

3 Bring to the boil, cover with a lid, lower the heat and simmer gently for 1 hour. Serve with creamed potato and cauliflower.

Vegetable soup with cheese dumplings

you will need:

1 lb. mixed diced vegetables (carrots, onion, celery, swede or potato)	**for the cheese dumplings:**
	4 oz. self-raising flour
	salt
1 tablespoon lentils (soaked for 2–3 hours)	2 oz. shredded beef suet
	1½ oz. grated Cheddar cheese
1 pint water	water to mix
½ level teaspoon salt	
1 level tablespoon flour	
cold water to mix	**to garnish:**
	chopped parsley

1 Prepare the vegetables and place in a large saucepan with the soaked lentils, water and salt.

2 Bring to the boil, cover and simmer gently for 1½ hours.

3 In a small basin blend the flour with sufficient cold water to make a thin paste and stir into soup. Stir until boiling and slightly thickened. Rub soup through a sieve and return to the pan.

4 To prepare the dumplings, sieve the flour and salt into a basin. Add the suet, and cheese and stir in sufficient cold water to mix to a firm dough. Divide into 8 portions.

5 With lightly floured hands shape each portion into a ball and add to the simmering soup. Cover and simmer for 20 minutes.

6 Sprinkle with chopped parsley and serve the soup immediately.

Oxtail stew

you will need:

1–1½ lb. oxtail cut at the joints	½ oz. dripping OR lard
bouquet garni	1 level tablespoon flour
1 onion, sliced	salt and pepper
8 oz. carrots, sliced	1 teaspoon tomato purée
2 oz. turnip, sliced	Juice ½ lemon

1 Wash and dry the oxtail and finish cutting through at the joints. Place in a saucepan, cover with water, add *bouquet garni* and bring to the boil.

2 Cover and simmer for 2 hours. Strain off the liquid, allow this to cool, then skim off the heavy layer of fat.

3 Sauté the onion, carrot and turnip in the hot fat until browned, then place in a large casserole dish with the oxtail.

4 Stir the flour into the hot fat and cook, stirring occasionally, until browned. Gradually stir in the 1 pint of the oxtail cooking broth and bring to the boil. Season well and add the tomato purée.

5 Strain over the contents of the casserole, cover and either simmer gently on top of the stove for a further 1½–2 hours, or place in the centre of a very moderate oven (350°F. – Gas Mark 3) and cook for 2–3 hours, or until the meat is tender and easily comes off the bone. Add lemon juice and serve with parsley potatoes.

Chilli con carne

you will need:

2 tablespoons cooking oil	1 8-oz. tin baked beans in tomato sauce
1 small onion, finely sliced	1 green pepper, sliced
2 oz. mushrooms, sliced	¼ level teaspoon chilli powder
8 oz. minced beef	pinch cayenne pepper
1 rounded teaspoon flour	¼ level teaspoon paprika
1 8-oz. tin tomatoes	8 oz. long grain rice for serving

1 Heat the oil and add the onion and mushrooms. Fry gently 2–3 minutes to soften, then add the meat and brown.

2 Stir in the flour and then the tomatoes plus liquid from the tin, beans, green pepper and spices.

3 Bring to the boil, lower the heat, cover and simmer for 1 hour. Sprinkle the rice into boiling salted water and cook rapidly for 10 minutes until tender. Drain and serve with the chilli con carne and tossed salad or green vegetables.

Beef goulash

you will need:

12 oz. buttock steak or chuck steak	salt and pepper
8 oz. onions, peeled and sliced	1 level tablespoon flour
1–2 cloves garlic, crushed	¾ pint beef stock OR water plus stock cube
1 level teaspoon caraway seeds	2 teaspoons tomato purée
1 level tablespoon paprika	⅛ pint sour cream OR yoghurt

1 Wipe the meat and cut away any fat. Chop the fat into small pieces and heat in a heavy frying pan until the fat runs. Add a little extra dripping if necessary. Remove lumps of fat from the pan. Cut the meat into neat cubes, add to the pan and brown.

2 Add the onions with the garlic, caraway seeds paprika and plenty of seasoning.

3 Cover with a tight-fitting lid and cook gently for 1 hour. Shake and stir occasionally.

4 Sprinkle the flour over the meat and stir in the stock and tomato purée. Bring to the boil, cover and simmer for a further hour, stirring occasionally.

5 Check the seasoning and, just before serving stir in the sour cream or yoghurt.

6 Serve with buttered noodles or boiled potatoes tossed in butter.

Beef and bean bake

you will need:

1 onion, finely chopped	**for the crumble topping:**
1 oz. butter OR margarine	3 oz. plain flour
1 11-oz. tin stewing steak	2 oz. butter OR margarine
1 8-oz. tin baked beans in tomato sauce	2 oz. finely grated Cheddar cheese
½ teaspoon made mustard	
1 teaspoon Worcestershire sauce	

1 Lightly fry the onion in the hot fat for about 5 minutes to soften.

2 Add the stewed steak, removing top layer of fat first from the tin, baked beans, mustard and sauce. Bring slowly to the boil, stirring only to blend the ingredients.

3 Draw the pan off the heat and pour the mixture into a 1–1½ pint pie or casserole dish. Prepare crumble topping.

4 Sift the flour into a mixing basin and rub in the fat. Add grated cheese and mix lightly with a fork.

5 Sprinkle the crumble over the beef and bean mixture. Place the casserole in the centre of a hot oven (400°F. – Gas Mark 6) and bake for

30 minutes or until top is crisp and contents bubbling hot.

6 Serve with grilled tomatoes.

Chicken stew with onions

you will need:

2 chicken joints
8 oz. button or small onions, peeled and left whole
1 pint stock OR water plus stock cube

1 oz. butter OR margarine
1 level tablespoon flour
salt and pepper
squeeze lemon juice

1 Trim the chicken joints and place in a saucepan with the onions. Cover with the stock, bring to the boil and simmer for 1–1½ hours, until the chicken and onions are tender.
2 Strain the chicken broth from the chicken and onion (keep these hot, on one side) into a saucepan and boil rapidly to reduce until about ¼ pint.
3 Melt the butter or margarine in a saucepan and stir in the flour. Cook gently for 1 minute.
4 Gradually beat in the chicken broth, stirring well all the time to get a smooth sauce. Bring to the boil and simmer gently for 2–3 minutes.
5 Season and stir in the lemon juice. Add the chicken and onion and heat through. Pour into a hot serving dish, and serve with sauté potatoes, and buttered broccoli spears.

Curried veal with rice

you will need:

12 oz. lean veal
1 oz. butter OR margarine
1 onion, finely chopped
1 level tablespoon flour
2 level tablespoons curry powder
¼ pint stock OR water plus stock cube

1 tablespoon sweet chutney
1 tablespoon brown sugar
juice ½ lemon
salt and pepper
6 oz. long grain rice

1 Trim the veal and cut into neat cubes. Fry in the hot butter to brown, then place in a casserole dish.
2 Add the onion to the hot butter and sauté for about 5 minutes until soft. Stir in the flour and curry powder and the stock, bring to the boil.
3 Add the chutney (with any large pieces chopped up), brown sugar and lemon juice and pour over the veal in the casserole. Season.
4 Cover and place in the centre of a very moderate oven (335°F. – Gas Mark 3) and cook for 2 hours.
5 Meanwhile add the rice to plenty of boiling salted water and cook rapidly for 10 minutes until tender. Drain and return to a hot saucepan for 5 minutes to steam dry.
6 Serve the hot rice as a base and spoon over the curried veal.

Crab corn bake

you will need:

1 small (3¼-oz.) tin crab meat
1 7-oz. tin whole kernel sweet corn
1 small onion, finely chopped
1 oz. butter OR margarine
1 level tablespoon flour
⅓ pint (or 1 teacupful) milk
1 teaspoon made mustard

1 teaspoon Worcestershire sauce
salt and pepper

for the topping:
½ oz. butter OR margarine
1 rounded tablespoon fresh white breadcrumbs
1 oz. grated Cheddar cheese

1 Place the crab meat (removing any sinews) in the base of a 1 pint baking or casserole dish along with the drained corn and prepared onion.
2 Melt the butter or margarine over moderate heat and stir in the flour. Cook for 1 minute, then gradually add the milk beating well to get a smooth sauce.
3 Add the mustard, Worcestershire sauce and season well with salt and pepper. Cook gently for 1 minute then pour over the crab and corn mixture. Set aside while preparing the topping.
4 Melt the butter, then draw the pan off the heat and using a fork stir in the crumbs and cheese. Toss until crumbs are buttery and then sprinkle over the top of the casserole.
5 Place in the centre of a fairly hot oven (380°F. – Gas Mark 5) and bake for 20–25 minutes until top is crispy and brown. Serve with grilled tomatoes and sauté potatoes.

Scallops au gratin

you will need:

2 large scallops
⅓ pint milk
lemon slices
salt and pepper
2 oz. butter OR margarine
1 level tablespoon flour

3 oz. grated Cheddar cheese
1 heaped tablespoon fresh white breadcrumbs

to garnish:
chopped parsley

1 Ask the fishmonger to open the scallops for you, and remove the 'beard'. Ask also for the shell (the deep half) and use as a serving dish.
2 Cut the prepared, washed scallops into 6 or 8 pieces and place in a saucepan with the milk, lemon slices and seasoning.
3 Bring to the boil, then lower the heat and poach for 15–20 minutes. Then drain off the cooking liquor, reserving this for the sauce, and discard lemon slices.
4 Melt 1 oz. of the butter in a saucepan over low heat and stir in the flour. Cook gently for 1 minute, then gradually beat in the cooking liquor, stirring well all the time to get a smooth

sauce. Bring to the boil, check seasoning and cook for 2–3 minutes.

5 Add the cooked scallops and 2 oz. of the cheese. Heat through and then spoon into the scallops shells.

6 Melt the remaining butter over low heat, draw the pan off the heat, stir in the breadcrumbs with a fork. When the butter is absorbed add reserved cheese, sprinkle over the scallops.

7 Place on a baking tray, and set above centre in a moderate oven (355°F. – Gas Mark 4) and bake for 15 minutes or until bubbling and browned. Sprinkle with chopped parsley.

Baked stuffed pork chops

you will need:

2 pork chops	1 heaped tablespoon fresh white bread-crumbs
for the stuffing:	1 dessertspoon chopped parsley
1 oz. butter	
½ small onion, finely chopped	pinch mixed herbs
	2 back bacon rashers

1 Trim away any rind and excess fat from the pork chops and place in a casserole dish. Set aside while preparing the filling.

2 Melt the butter in a small pan and add the onion. Fry gently for about 5 minutes until soft then draw the pan off the heat.

3 Using a fork, stir in the breadcrumbs, parsley and herbs and mix well until the crumbs have absorbed all the butter.

4 Heap the stuffing on to the pork chops and top with a trimmed bacon rasher.

5 Add 2 tablespoons water to the casserole dish, cover with a lid and place in a moderate oven (355°F. – Gas Mark 4) and bake 1½ hours.

6 Serve with creamed potatoes and green peas.

Liver casserole with bacon dumplings

you will need:

8 oz. calf's liver, sliced	**for the bacon dumplings:**
seasoned flour	
1 oz. butter OR margarine for frying	4 oz. self-raising flour
3 carrots, sliced	1 level teaspoon grated lemon rind
1 onion, sliced	2 oz. shredded beef suet
1–2 stalks celery, sliced	
¼ pint stock OR water plus stock cube	2 rashers bacon, trimmed and chopped
pinch mixed herbs	3 tablespoons water
salt and pepper	squeeze lemon juice

1 Trim the liver and dip in seasoned flour. Brown quickly in hot butter.

2 Arrange the liver and prepared vegetables in a casserole dish, beginning and ending with a layer of vegetables.

3 Pour on the hot stock, add the herbs and seasoning. Cover and place in the centre of a very moderate oven (355°F. – Gas Mark 4) and cook for 1½ hours.

4 To prepare the bacon dumplings, sift the flour into a small basin. Add the lemon rind, suet and bacon and mix to a firm dough with the water and lemon juice. Divide into 8 portions.

5 With lightly floured hands, shape each portion into a ball. Add the dumplings to the liver casserole, placing them on top of the nearly cooked vegetables and meat.

6 Cover and continue cooking for 30 minutes. Serve at once.

Lamb cutlets with tomatoes

you will need:

2 lamb cutlets	1 8-oz. tin tomatoes
1 oz. dripping	salt and pepper
1 onion, finely chopped	

1 Trim the cutlets and brown quickly in the hot fat.

2 Add the onion, tomatoes plus liquid from the tin, and seasoning.

3 Cover with a lid and simmer gently for 1 hour.

4 Lift the cutlets from the pan and place on a hot serving dish. Rub the contents of the saucepan through a sieve to make a sauce. Check the seasoning, and spoon sauce over the lamb cutlets. Serve with creamed potato.

Individual steak and kidney puddings

you will need:

8 oz. steak and kidney	**for the suet pastry:**
seasoned flour	6 oz. self-raising flour
½ oz. dripping or vegetable shortening	¼ level teaspoon salt
½ onion, finely chopped	3 oz. shredded beef suet
¼ pint stock OR water plus stock cube	water to mix
2 oz. mushrooms, trimmed and chopped	

1 Trim any fat or gristle away from the meat and cut in small cubes. Roll in seasoned flour and brown in hot fat.

2 Sprinkle over a little of the seasoned flour to help thicken the gravy, add the onion and stir in the hot stock.

3 Bring to the boil, add the mushrooms and simmer gently for 1½ hours. Draw the pan off the heat and prepare the suet pastry.

4 Sift the flour and salt into a basin. Add the suet and stir in enough water to mix to a firm dough.

5 Turn out on to a lightly floured working

surface and knead lightly to a smooth dough. Divide into two portions.

6 Roll each piece of dough out to a circle large enough to line a buttered ½-pint pudding basin (use kitchen teacups as an alternative). Cut out a quarter of the circle and set aside for the lids.

7 Line the basins or cups with remaining dough, sealing cut edges together. Fill each with a little of the cooked meat mixture and a little gravy. Roll out remaining pastry pieces, damp edges and cover the puddings.

8 Press edges down well to seal, cover first with double-thickness greased greaseproof paper – fold in a pleat to allow for expansion, then cover with a square of kitchen foil.

9 Steam briskly for 1 hour, turn out and serve with gravy and green beans.

Rabbit hot pot

you will need:

1 lb. rabbit pieces	2 carrots, sliced
seasoned flour	2 stalks celery, sliced
1 oz. dripping OR	¾ pint stock OR water
vegetable shortening	plus stock cube
1 onion, sliced	salt and pepper

1 Wipe the rabbit pieces and roll in seasoned flour.

2 Brown quickly in the hot fat, then place in a casserole dish.

3 Add the onion, carrot and celery to the casserole. Sprinkle a little of the seasoned flour over the hot fat in the pan and stir over moderate heat until frothy and brown.

4 Gradually stir in the stock and bring to the boil. Check seasoning and strain over the rabbit and vegetables.

5 Place in the centre of a moderate oven (355°F. – Gas Mark 4) and cook for 1½–2 hours, or until the rabbit meat slides easily off the bone.

6 Serve with creamed potatoes.

Fried liver with onion sauce

you will need:

8 oz. calf's liver, sliced	½ pint stock OR water
seasoned flour	plus stock cube
1 oz. butter OR	salt and pepper
margarine	
2 medium-sized onions,	
cut in rings	

1 Trim the liver and dip in seasoned flour. Fry quickly in the hot fat 3–5 minutes, turning to brown evenly. Lift from the pan on to a hot serving dish.

2 Add the onions to the frying pan and cook over moderate heat for 5 minutes or until soft. Sprinkle in about 1 level tablespoon of the seasoned flour and fry, stirring, until frothy and brown.

3 Gradually stir in the stock and bring to the boil. Check seasoning and simmer 1 minute.

4 Pour the sauce on the liver and serve with creamed potato and a green vegetable.

Hampshire bacon dumplings

you will need:

6 oz. self-raising flour	¼ level teaspoon mixed
½ level teaspoon salt	herbs
pinch pepper	1 level tablespoon
4 oz. shredded beef	chopped parsley
suet	4 oz. bacon rashers,
2 oz. fresh white	trimmed and
breadcrumbs	chopped
1 small onion, finely	approximately ¼ pint
chopped	water

1 Sift the flour and salt into a basin. Add remaining ingredients and mix to a firm dough with the water.

2 Turn the mixture on to a lightly floured working surface and with floured hands shape into a fat roll.

3 Wrap first in double-thickness greased greaseproof paper (folded in a pleat to allow for expansion) and tie like a cracker at each end. Then wrap loosely in kitchen foil.

4 Steam briskly for 1½ hours. Remove papers, slice and serve with grilled tomatoes and gravy.

Pork chops Italiano

you will need:

2 spare-rib pork chops	2 oz. mushrooms
salt and pepper	1 small green pepper,
1 tablespoon salad oil	seeded and sliced
1 small onion, sliced	1 bay leaf
1 small tin cream of	juice ½ lemon
tomato soup	

1 Trim the chops and season. Heat the oil in a saucepan and brown the chops on both sides then remove from the pan.

2 Add the onion, cook gently until tender and lightly browned.

3 Replace the chops and add the soup, mushrooms, green pepper, bay leaf and lemon juice, Cover and simmer gently for 1 hour.

4 When cooked remove the bay leaf and check seasoning. Serve the chops with the sauce poured over, and accompany with creamed potatoes and French beans.

Beefsteak casserole with dumpling top

you will need:

12 oz. stewing steak	½ soup can water
seasoned flour	
½ oz. dripping OR	**for the dumpling top:**
vegetable shortening	4 oz. self-raising flour
1 onion, sliced	pinch salt
2 carrots, sliced	2 oz. shredded beef
2 stalks celery,	suet
chopped	water to mix
1 small tin condensed	
tomato soup	

1 Remove any fat or gristle from the meat and cut the meat into neat pieces. Roll in seasoned flour.
2 Heat the fat in a medium-sized saucepan, add the meat and brown over moderate heat. Lift the meat from the pan and add the vegetables. Fry gently but do not brown.
3 Replace the meat in the pan, add the soup and water and check seasoning.
4 Cover the pan and simmer very gently for 1½ hours, stirring occasionally.
5 Meanwhile, to prepare the dumpling top, sift the flour and salt into a basin, add the suet and enough water to mix to a firm dough.
6 Turn out on to a lightly floured working surface and pat out to a circle approximately the size of the pan. Remove the lid and place the dough on top of the meat. Replace the lid and continue to simmer for a further ¾–1 hour until the dumpling top is risen and cooked.
7 Cut the dumpling into half, and serve with the meat, vegetables and gravy straight from the saucepan.

Creamed ham and mushrooms

you will need:

2 oz. butter OR	4 oz. cooked ham, cut
margarine	in one thick slice
1 level tablespoon flour	6 oz. long grain rice
¼ pint milk	1 oz. grated Parmesan
salt and pepper	cheese
4 oz. button mush-	
rooms	

1 Melt half the butter or margarine in a saucepan over moderate heat and stir in the flour. Cook gently for 1 minute, then gradually stir in the milk, beating well to make a smooth sauce.
2 Bring to the boil, season and cook gently for 2–3 minutes.
3 Heat the remaining butter in a small frying pan and add the mushrooms. Fry rapidly for 2–3 minutes, then draw off the heat.
4 Add cooked mushrooms and ham cut in dice to the sauce, and allow to heat through gently.

5 Meanwhile, to prepare the rice ring, sprinkle the rice into plenty of boiling salted water, cook rapidly for 10 minutes until tender, drain and pack firmly into a buttered ring mould.
6 Turn the moulded rice out immediately on to a hot serving platter and spoon the creamed ham and mushroom sauce into this centre. Sprinkle with grated Parmesan cheese and serve with tossed salad.

Stuffed cabbage

you will need:

4 large cabbage leaves	½ level teaspoon salt
(use outer leaves)	pinch pepper
	2 oz. mushrooms,
for the stuffing:	peeled and chopped
1 oz. butter OR	
margarine	1 tin condensed tomato
½ onion, finely chopped	soup
8 oz. minced beef	4 tablespoons water

1 Blanch the cabbage leaves in boiling water for 2–3 minutes to soften them.
2 Meanwhile to prepare the stuffing, melt the butter or margarine in a saucepan, add onion and sauté gently until soft. Add mince, seasoning and mushrooms and cook, stirring gently until the mince is browned all over.
3 Place a portion of stuffing in the centre of each leaf. Fold the sides over and roll leaves up so that the stuffing is completely enclosed.
4 Place in a greased casserole dish and pour over the blended soup and water. Cover and place in the centre of a very moderate oven (355°F. – Gas Mark 4) and bake until tender (about 40 minutes).
5 Serve topped with a little parsley and hand crusty French bread separately.

Apple and banana crumble

you will need:

2 oz. plain flour	1 large apple
1 oz. butter OR	1 banana
margarine	1 tablespoon water
1 level tablespoon	
castor sugar	

1 Sift the flour into a basin and rub in the butter or margarine. Add the sugar and continue to rub in until the mixture begins to cling together in lumps. Set aside while preparing the filling.
2 Peel, core and slice the apple into a buttered 1-pint pie or baking dish. Peel and slice the banana and add to the apple with the water.
3 Top with the crumble mixture, spreading it evenly and pressing down lightly.
4 Place in the centre of a moderate oven (355°F. – Gas Mark 4) and bake for 30–35 minutes. Serve with cream or top of the milk. *continued*

Variations

Gooseberry crumble – prepare the crumble mixture as given before. Place 8 oz. topped and tailed green gooseberries, 2 oz. castor sugar and 1 tablespoon water in the pie dish. Cover with the crumble mixture and bake as directed.

Rhubarb crumble – prepare the crumble mixture as given before. Place 8 oz. fresh rhubarb cut in short lengths, 2 oz. soft brown sugar and a pinch of ground ginger in the pie dish. Cover with the crumble mixture and bake as directed.

Fruit float

you will need:

1 7-oz. tin peach slices	1 oz. castor sugar
½ pint milk	
2 level tablespoons	**to decorate:**
custard powder	chopped walnuts

1 Put the fruit and juice into two individual glass serving dishes.
2 Measure the milk into a saucepan. In a basin blend the custard powder with enough milk taken from the pan to make a thin paste.
3 Bring the milk almost to the boil, then draw off the heat and stir into the custard blend. Return the mixture to the saucepan and bring to the boil stirring all the time.
4 Add the sugar and cook for 1 minute. Draw the pan off the heat and allow the custard to cool, stirring occasionally to prevent a skin forming.
5 Pour over the fruit, allowing the fruit juice to float up round the sides. Sprinkle with chopped walnuts and serve.

Marmalade glazed pears

you will need:

2 level tablespoons	**for the glaze:**
custard powder	1 heaped tablespoon
½ pint milk	marmalade
1 oz. castor sugar	1 tablespoon water
1 7-oz. tin pears	1 tablespoon castor
	sugar

1 Blend the custard powder with a little of the milk to make a thin paste. Heat remaining milk until almost boiling and pour over the custard blend. Stir well and return to the milk saucepan.
2 Stir over moderate heat until thickened and boiling. Draw the pan off the heat and stir in the castor sugar.
3 Allow to cool a few moments then pour into the base of two individual glass serving dishes.
4 Top with the pears drained from the juice.
5 In a saucepan combine together the ingredients for the glaze. Stir over low heat to dissolve the sugar and then bring up to the boil and cook for

2–3 minutes until syrupy. Draw the pan off the heat and cool before pouring over the pears.
6 Serve warm with cream or top of the milk.

Apple sponge

you will need:

8 oz. cooking apples	2 trifle sponge cakes
1–2 level tablespoons	1 egg
castor sugar	¼ pint milk

1 Peel, quarter and core the apples. Slice thinly and place in the base of a shallow 1 pint baking dish. Sprinkle with the sugar.
2 Slice each sponge cake in half across and arrange over the apples cut side down.
3 Whisk together the egg and milk and strain over the sponge cakes.
4 Place in the centre of a moderate oven (350°F. – Gas Mark 4) and bake for 30–40 minutes.

Steamed jam pudding

you will need:

3 oz. self-raising flour	**for the sauce:**
2 oz. butter OR	1 tablespoon red jam
margarine	1 tablespoon castor
2 oz. castor sugar	sugar
1 egg	1 tablespoon water
milk to mix	
1 dessertspoon red jam	

1 Well butter a 1–1½ pint pudding basin, and set aside while preparing the pudding.
2 Sift the flour on to a square of paper. Cream the butter and sugar until light, gradually beat in the lightly mixed egg, adding a little of the sieved flour with the last of the egg.
3 Fold in remaining flour and enough milk to mix a medium soft consistency.
4 Place a tablespoon of red jam in the base of the prepared pudding basin, and spoon sponge mixture on top.
5 Cover with double thickness of greased grease-proof paper (fold in a pleat to allow for expansion) and tie tightly. Cover with an extra square of kitchen foil for extra protection.
6 Steam briskly for 1 hour. Remove papers and serve immediately with jam sauce.
7 To make the sauce, combine the jam, sugar and water in a small saucepan and bring to the boil slowly to dissolve the sugar, then boil briskly until thick and syrupy.

Variation

Marmalade pudding – follow the recipe given above using 1 dessertspoon orange marmalade instead of jam in the pudding bowl. Prepare the sauce, using 1 good tablespoon sieved orange marmalade; include the peel if a finely shredded marmalade is used.

Lemon rice meringue

you will need:

¾ pint milk
2 level tablespoons round grain (pudding) rice
finely grated rind ½ lemon
2 oz. castor sugar
1 egg

1 Measure the milk into a saucepan and bring to the boil. Add rice, cover with a lid, simmer gently for 30–50 minutes or until rice is tender and creamy, stir occasionally to avoid sticking.
2 Stir in the lemon rind, half the sugar and the egg yolk. Pour into a buttered 1–pint baking or pie dish.

3 In a basin whisk the egg white until stiff, then gradually whisk in the remaining sugar. Spoon the meringue over the top of the rice pudding.
4 Place above centre in a moderately hot oven (380°F. – Gas Mark 5) until browned. Serve at once with cream or top of the milk.

Variation

Orange rice meringue – follow the recipe given above, using the finely grated rind of 1 small orange instead of lemon. Add 1 tablespoon seedless raisins with the sugar and egg yolk. Finish and bake as directed above.

For special occasions

Birthdays . . . anniversaries . . . there are many occasions when something a little more exotic, less every-day, is required. Here are some ideas, not necessarily more difficult to prepare, that are just right when it's a party for two.

Mushroom consommé

you will need:

½ oz. butter OR margarine
½ small onion, finely chopped
3–4 oz. mushrooms, trimmed and sliced
1 pint stock OR water plus chicken stock cube
squeeze of lemon juice
1 tablespoon sherry

1 Melt the butter in a saucepan and gently fry the onion until tender and lightly brown. Add the mushrooms and fry a further 5 minutes.
2 Add the stock and lemon juice and bring just up to the boil.
3 Draw the pan off the heat, check the seasoning, stir in the sherry and serve with cheese straws.

Cheese straws

you will need:

4 oz. plain flour
pinch salt and cayenne pepper
2 oz. mixed vegetable shortening and butter
2 oz. finely grated Parmesan cheese
2–3 tablespoons mixed egg and milk
paprika pepper for decoration

1 Sift the flour, salt and cayenne into a mixing basin. Add the blended fats and rub in. Add the cheese and stir in enough beaten egg and milk to mix to a firm dough.
2 Turn out on to a lightly floured board and roll the dough out about ¼ inch thick. From one corner cut out about six 1½ inch rings – using a pastry cutter.
3 Cut remaining pastry into 2 inch strips and then into thin straws.

4 Place straws and rings on a greased baking tray and place in the centre of a hot oven (400°F. – Gas Mark 6). Bake for 8–10 minutes or until pale golden brown.
5 While still warm, dip the ends of the straws in paprika pepper and slip into the rings to make bundles. Serve with clear soups or with cocktail snacks.

Poached salmon cutlets with cucumber sauce

you will need:

2 salmon cutlets
½ pint water
1 lemon, sliced
½ level teaspoon salt
1 bay leaf
for the cucumber sauce:
½ cucumber
1 oz. butter
1 rounded tablespoon flour
¼ pint milk
salt and pepper
1–2 tablespoons cream

1 Snip away the fins from the cutlets and place in a large saucepan. Add water, lemon, salt and bay leaf.
2 Bring slowly to the boil, then lower the heat at once, cover and poach very gently 1 minute. Draw the pan off the heat and leave cutlets in the water until ready to serve.
3 Meanwhile, to prepare the sauce, peel the cucumber, cut in half lengthways, remove the seeds and then slice.
4 Melt the butter in a small saucepan, add the cucumber and cook over gentle heat covered with a lid, for 5 minutes or until the cucumber is softened.
5 Add the flour and then gradually stir in the milk. Bring to the boil and simmer gently for 2–3 minutes. Draw the pan off the heat, season and add the cream – the sauce should be fairly thin.
6 Lift the salmon from the cooking liquor on to

a warm serving platter, pour over the sauce and garnish with lemon slices. Serve with parsley potatoes and grilled mushrooms.

Chicken marengo

you will need:

1 onion, chopped	¾ pint stock OR water
1 carrot, sliced	plus stock cube
2 bacon rashers,	salt and pepper
chopped	4 oz. mushrooms
2 oz. butter OR	2 chicken joints
margarine	seasoned flour
1 oz. plain flour	2 tablespoons dry
1 teaspoon tomato	sherry
purée	

1 Prepare the vegetables and bacon and sauté gently in half the butter until golden brown and soft (about 10 minutes).
2 Stir in the flour and continue to cook gently, stirring occasionally, until the flour is a rich nutty brown colour.
3 Add the tomato purée and gradually stir in the hot stock. Bring to the boil, season and add mushroom stalks, reserving caps for later.
4 Cover and simmer gently for 30 minutes,
5 Meanwhile trim the chicken joints and roll in seasoned flour. Brown on both sides in remaining butter, then drain and place in a casserole dish. Add the sliced mushroom caps.
6 Draw the pan of sauce off the heat and strain into the casserole over the chicken. Add the sherry, cover and place in the centre of a very moderate oven (355°F. – Gas Mark 4). Bake for 1 hour or until the chicken is tender.
7 Serve the chicken with sauce over, with rissole potatoes and buttered broccoli spears.

Chicken with orange and almond sauce

you will need:

2 chicken joints	1 oz. blanched
salt and pepper	almonds, sliced and
1 oz. butter	toasted
¼ pint (or 1 teacup)	
orange juice – use	
tinned	

1 Trim the chicken joints and season with salt and pepper.
2 Fry in the hot butter quickly to brown on both sides. Then cover the pan with a lid, lower the heat and fry for a further 25–30 minutes until the chicken is tender.
3 Remove the cooked chicken joints from the pan on to a hot serving platter, pour away all but 1 tablespoon of fat from the frying pan and stir in the orange juice.

4 Bring up to the boil and cook rapidly until reduced by half. Stir in the almonds and then pour over the chicken joints.
5 Serve with broccoli spears and sauté potatoes.

Beef Stroganoff

you will need:

8 oz. fillet steak	4 oz. button
black pepper	mushrooms, sliced
squeeze lemon juice	2 oz. butter
1 small onion, finely	1 carton soured cream
chopped	4–6 oz. long grain rice

1 Trim the meat and cut into very thin strips about 2 inches long, ¼ inch thick. Sprinkle with a little freshly ground black pepper and a squeeze of lemon juice and leave to marinate for 30 minutes.
2 Sauté onion and mushrooms over low heat in half the butter until soft (about 5 minutes). Do not allow to brown.
3 Melt the remaining butter in a frying pan and quickly brown the meat, turning to seal on all sides. Stir in the soured cream and add the onion and mushrooms.
4 Meanwhile sprinkle the rice into a pan of boiling salted water and cook briskly for 10 minutes. Drain and serve the hot rice along with the beef Stroganoff and a tossed salad.

Veal in white wine sauce

you will need:

12 oz. veal fillet OR	¼ pint stock OR water
stewing veal	plus stock cube
1 oz. butter OR	¼ pint dry white wine
margarine	salt and pepper
1 small onion, sliced	2–3 tablespoons cream
1 level tablespoon flour	

to garnish:
chopped parsley

1 Trim away any fat or gristle from the veal and cut the meat into neat pieces.
2 Heat the butter and fry to seal the meat but do not allow to brown. Lift from the pan and keep hot.
3 Add the onion to the hot butter and fry gently until soft but do not allow to brown. Stir in the flour and then gradually add the stock and white wine, stirring well to make a smooth sauce.
4 Add seasoning if liked and replace the meat in the sauce.
5 Bring up to the boil, cover and cook gently for 1–1½ hours, or until tender.
6 Draw the pan off the heat and stir in the cream. Sprinkle with chopped parsley and serve with duchesse potatoes and buttered broccoli spears.

Pork fillet with mushrooms

you will need:

8 oz. pork fillet
seasoned flour
1 oz. butter
½ onion, finely chopped
4 oz. mushrooms,
   trimmed and sliced

¼ pint single cream
squeeze lemon juice
1 teaspoon chopped
   parsley

Cut the fillet across in 1-inch-thick slices, beat flat and roll in seasoned flour.

Heat the butter in a frying pan and add the onion. Fry gently over low heat until the onion is soft (about 5 minutes).

Add the pork and mushrooms, and cook for 5–6 minutes until the mushrooms are soft and the pork browned. Stir in the cream and *heat only until almost boiling.*

Draw the pan off the heat and stir in the lemon juice and parsley.

Serve at once with creamed potatoes and buttered broccoli spears.

Stuffed pork chops

you will need:

2 pork chops, cut at
   least ½ inch thick
salt and pepper
1 small tin pâté de foie
1 small egg, lightly
   mixed

2–3 rounded table-
   spoons fresh white
   breadcrumbs
½ oz. lard for frying

Using a sharp knife, cut away any rind from the chops, slit each one lengthwise from the outside edge into the bone and make a pocket.

Season inside and out then stuff the pocket with pâté. Press down lightly to reshape the chop.

Dip each chop first in lightly mixed egg, then in the breadcrumbs and pat on firmly to make a good coating.

Fry quickly in the hot fat to brown both sides, then cover with a lid and cook the chops, turning occasionally, for 30 minutes.

Remove the lid 10 minutes before the end of the cooking time to crisp the outside of the chops.

Drain and serve with buttered asparagus tips and parsley potatoes.

Coq au vin

you will need:

2 chicken joints
seasoned flour
1 oz. butter OR
   margarine
1 clove garlic
2 bacon rashers
4 button onions, peeled
   and left whole

4 button mushrooms,
   trimmed
½ pint white stock OR
   water plus stock cube
¼ pint red wine
bouquet garni

Trim the chicken joints and roll in seasoned flour. Fry in the hot butter to brown on both sides, then drain and place in a casserole. Either rub the crushed garlic round the inside of dish first to give a little flavour, then discard or, for stronger flavour, chop and add to casserole.

2 Add the trimmed and chopped bacon, onions and mushrooms, stock, red wine and *bouquet garni.*

3 Cover with a lid and place in the centre of a moderate oven (350°F. – Gas Mark 3) and cook for 1 hour.

4 Serve the chicken joints with the vegetables, creamed potatoes and green beans.

For a thick sauce – if a thick sauce is preferred, blend stock well with 1 level teaspoon cornflour and stir over moderate heat until thick and boiling. Then pour over chicken and vegetables and serve.

Grilled poussin

you will need:

1 small poussin —
   about 1 lb.
1 oz. butter

salt and freshly milled
   pepper
4 lean bacon rashers

1 Using a sharp knife cut the bird open down the backbone so that it lies flat.

2 Place inside upwards on the grill pan and spread the surface liberally with the butter. Season with salt and pepper.

3 Place under a preheated hot grill and cook for 20–25 minutes turning after 10 minutes. Baste the second side with the melted butter in the grill pan.

4 About 5 minutes before the cooking time is complete, place the trimmed bacon rashers alongside the chicken.

5 When cooked, separate the two halves of chicken and serve with the bacon rashers.

Sweet and sour pork

you will need:

12 oz. pork fillet
1 oz. lard OR shorten-
   ing for frying

**for the sweet and
sour sauce:**
1 8-oz. tin pineapple
   rings

4 tablespoons vinegar
3 oz. soft brown sugar
1 tablespoon soy sauce
¼ level teaspoon salt
2 level tablespoons
   cornflour
1 small green pepper,
   thinly sliced

1 Cut away any fat from the meat and cut meat into cubes. Fry in the hot fat until golden brown on all sides. Set aside while preparing the sweet and sour sauce.

2 Drain the pineapple from the tin and reserve the syrup, making it up to ½ pint with water. Combine this with the vinegar, brown sugar, soy sauce and salt. *continued*

3 Measure the cornflour into a saucepan, mix to a thin paste with a little of the liquid then stir in the remaining liquid.
4 Simmer over moderate heat, stirring constantly until thickened and clear.
5 Add the meat, cover and cook for 1 hour or until the meat is tender. Add the sliced pepper and pineapple cut in chunks and cook a further 15 minutes.
6 Serve with boiled or fried rice, bean sprouts and crispy noodles.

Fried rice

Heat 1 tablespoon oil in a saucepan and add 1 finely chopped onion and 6 oz. long grain rice. Fry until the rice is golden brown then stir in ¾ pint hot stock or water plus stock cube. Bring to the boil, then simmer gently, covered for 20 minutes until rice is tender and liquid absorbed.

Blanquette of veal

you will need:

1 lb. stewing lean veal	1 rounded tablespoon
1 onion, chopped	flour
1–2 carrots, sliced	1 egg yolk
¾ pint chicken stock OR	2 tablespoons cream
water plus stock cube	
salt and pepper	2–4 oz. mushrooms,
small bay leaf	sliced
	½ oz. butter
for the sauce:	
1 oz. butter OR	**to garnish:**
margarine	chopped parsley

1 Trim away any gristle from the meat and cut into cubes. Blanch by plunging into boiling water for 2 minutes then drain.
2 Place the prepared vegetables in a saucepan and add the meat, stock, seasoning and bay leaf.
3 Bring to the boil and skim if necessary. Cover, lower the heat and cook gently for 1½ hours or until the meat is tender.
4 Draw the pan off the heat and remove the bay leaf. Strain the meat liquor off and reserve for the sauce. Keep the meat and vegetables hot in the saucepan or a casserole dish while preparing the sauce.
5 To make the sauce, melt the butter or margarine and stir in the flour. Cook over gentle heat for 1 minute but do not brown. Gradually stir in a generous ½ pint of the reserved meat liquor. Stir thoroughly until boiling, then cook gently for 5 minutes.
6 Check the seasoning and consistency – the sauce should thinly coat the back of a spoon. Draw the pan off the heat and stir in the egg yolk mixed with the cream.
7 Pour at once over the meat, add the mushrooms (sautéed in a little butter), sprinkle with chopped parsley and serve with boiled rice.

Variation

With rabbit – follow the recipe above using 1 lb. boned rabbit meat, in place of the veal.

Beef in red wine

you will need:

12 oz. stewing steak	4 oz. button mush-
seasoned flour	rooms, peeled and
1 oz. butter OR	sliced
margarine	pinch dried herbs
1 onion, sliced	salt and pepper
2 rashers streaky bacon	1 wine glass red wine
½ pint stock OR water	
plus stock cube	

1 Trim away fat and gristle from the meat and cut the meat into neat pieces. Toss in seasoned flour.
2 Melt the butter or margarine; add onion, meat, trimmed and chopped bacon rashers. Fry over moderate heat and brown slightly.
3 Remove the bacon and onion from the pan and place in a casserole dish.
4 Sprinkle a little of the seasoned flour into the hot butter, then stir in the stock and bring to the boil. Strain into the casserole dish, with the mushrooms, herbs, seasoning and red wine.
5 Cover and cook in the centre of a very moderate oven (355°F. – Gas Mark 4) for 2½–3 hours, or until the meat is tender.
6 Serve with parsley potatoes and green peas.

Chicken paprika

you will need:

1 oz. butter OR	1 level teaspoon salt
margarine	¾ pint chicken stock OR
1 small onion, finely	water plus stock cube
chopped	2 chicken joints
1 clove garlic, finely	¼ pint single cream
chopped	1 rounded tablespoon
1½ level tablespoons	flour
paprika	1 carton soured cream

1 In a heavy saucepan, melt the fat, add the onion and garlic and sauté gently until golden brown.
2 Add the paprika and salt and gradually stir in the stock. Bring to the boil, cover with a lid and simmer for 10 minutes.
3 Add the chicken joints, cover and simmer gently for about 1 hour or until the joints are tender.
4 Measure the cream into a small basin, sift the flour on to it and whisk thoroughly until blended.
5 Stir in a little of the boiling chicken stock, blend well and then return to the saucepan. Cook, stirring until thickened and boiling.
6 Draw the pan off the heat and stir in the soured cream. Serve the chicken paprika over plain boiled rice.

Kidneys in mustard cream sauce

you will need:

4 lambs' kidneys
1 teaspoon vinegar
2 oz. butter
salt and pepper
1 rounded teaspoon flour
¼ pint double cream
1–2 teaspoons prepared mustard

1 Remove fat from around the kidneys and snip out the core. Remove the skin and place the kidneys in a bowl with water to cover. Add the vinegar and leave to soak for 15 minutes.
2 Drain, pat dry and slice thickly.
3 Add to the hot butter in a frying pan and fry gently for 5 minutes.
4 Season with salt and pepper and sprinkle over the flour.
5 Stir in the cream and mustard to taste. Bring to the boil, stirring until thickened. Draw off the heat and serve.

Veal scaloppine

you will need:

2 veal escalopes
seasoned flour
1 oz. butter OR margarine
4 oz. mushrooms, sliced
¼ pint red wine

1 Ask your butcher to flatten the veal escalopes for you. Trim and then dip both sides in seasoned flour.
2 Heat the butter, add the veal and brown.
3 Lower the heat, add the mushrooms and cook gently for 2–3 minutes. Then stir in the wine, cover with a lid and simmer gently for 20 minutes.
4 Serve the veal with the mushrooms and sauce poured over, and accompanied by mashed potato and buttered green peas.

Marinated lamb chops

you will need:

2 loin or chump chops
fresh white bread-crumbs

for the marinade:
2 tablespoons salad oil

1 tablespoon dry cider or white wine
½ clove garlic, crushed and finely chopped
freshly milled black pepper

1 Trim the chops and set aside.
2 Combine all the ingredients for the marinade together in a shallow dish – take care to remove the outer papery coating from the garlic, and chop only the fleshy inner part. Add the chops and allow to marinate for 10 minutes, turning two or three times to flavour them well.
3 Drain the chops and dip in the breadcrumbs.
4 Pat coating on lightly and place under a pre-heated hot grill. Lower heat slightly and grill the chops for 3–5 minutes each side, according to thickness. Serve at once.

Lobster Mexicana

you will need:

1 7-oz. tin lobster meat
1 7-oz. tin whole kernel sweet corn
1 oz. butter
¼ pint single cream
salt and pepper
6 oz. long grain rice

1 Drain the lobster meat from the tin, remove any sinews and flake the flesh. Place in a saucepan with the drained corn and butter.
2 Place over low heat and stir occasionally until the butter has melted and the ingredients have warmed through.
3 Season well and add the cream. Heat thoroughly but do not allow to boil. Leave over very low heat while preparing the rice.
4 Sprinkle the rice into plenty of boiling salted water, cook briskly for 10 minutes until tender, then drain and turn into a hot dish. Dry in a warm oven for 2–3 minutes, then spoon the lobster sauce over and serve.

Scampi with parsley rice

you will need:

2 oz. butter OR margarine
1 small onion, finely chopped
1 8-oz. tin tomatoes
¼ pint dry white wine
pinch pepper
½ level teaspoon salt
1 rounded tablespoon flour
8 oz. prepared scampi
8 oz. long grain rice
1 tablespoon finely chopped parsley

1 Melt half the butter in a medium-sized sauce-pan and gently sauté the onion until soft.
2 Stir in the tomatoes, wine and seasoning. Cover and simmer gently for 10 minutes.
3 Cream remaining butter and flour, add to the ingredients and bring to the boil, stirring well until thickened.
4 Re-cover, cook gently for 5 minutes, then strain and return the sauce to the pan. Add scampi and simmer gently.
5 Meanwhile sprinkle the rice into plenty of boiling salted water, boil briskly for 8 minutes, drain and turn into a hot serving dish. Add the chopped parsley and toss with a fork. Heap rice into the centre of the dish.
6 Spoon the scampi sauce over the centre of the rice and serve at once with crusty French bread and butter.

Creamed lobster

you will need:

1 oz. butter
1 rounded tablespoon flour
¼ pint milk
salt and pepper
1 7-oz. tin lobster meat
1–2 tablespoons sherry
2 tablespoons double cream
cayenne pepper

for the topping:
½ oz. butter
1 heaped tablespoon fresh white bread-crumbs

1 Melt the butter in a saucepan over moderate heat. Stir in the flour and cook gently for 1 minute, but do not allow to brown.
2 Gradually stir in the milk, beating well all the time to get a really smooth sauce. Bring to the boil and cook gently 2–3 minutes.
3 Season to taste and add the flaked lobster flesh (with any sinews removed). Allow to heat.
4 Draw the pan off the heat, stir in the sherry and cream and add the cayenne pepper. Pour into 2 buttered ramekin dishes or 1 small buttered serving dish. Set in a warm place while preparing the topping.
5 Melt the butter in a small pan. Draw off the heat and add the breadcrumbs, stir with a fork until crumbs are buttery.
6 Spoon over the creamed lobster and brown under the grill. Serve with buttered toast and grilled tomatoes.

Sole with saffron rice

you will need:

1 small sole	1 egg yolk
salt and pepper	juice ½ lemon
¼ pint milk	1 level teaspoon sugar
mixed fish liquor and milk	pinch saffron
	6 oz. long grain rice
1 oz. butter OR margarine	
1 level tablespoon flour	**to garnish:** paprika

1 Ask the fishmonger to remove both skins from the sole and separate the fish into four fillets.
2 Season and roll up. Place in a buttered pie dish and pour the milk round the fish. Cover with a buttered paper and place in the centre of a very moderate oven (355°F. – Gas Mark 4) and bake for 15–20 minutes.
3 Drain the cooked fish and make drained cooking liquor up to ⅓ pint with extra milk if necessary. Keep the fish warm while preparing the sauce.
4 Melt the butter or margarine in a saucepan over low heat and stir in the flour. Gradually beat in the mixed fish liquor and milk and beat well to get a smooth sauce.
5 Season well and simmer gently for 2–3 minutes. Draw the pan off the heat and stir in the egg yolk, lemon juice and sugar.
6 Meanwhile add a pinch of saffron to boiling salted water, add the rice and cook briskly for 10 minutes until tender. Drain and spoon the rice over the base of a hot serving platter. Arrange the cooked fish on top and pour over the lemon sauce. Sprinkle with paprika.

Plaice with cheese sauce

you will need:

1 whole plaice	1 oz. butter OR margarine
salt and pepper	
½ onion, finely chopped	1 tablespoon flour
¼ pint milk	2–3 oz. grated Cheddar cheese

1 Have the fish filleted by fishmonger or, to separate yourself, use a sharp knife to loosen the skin; with fingers (dip in salt for a firm grip) hold the tail end of the fish towards you. Hold the knife at an angle with the blade sloping forwards and cut the skin away with a sawing movement.
2 Season the fish fillets fold in half and place in a well-buttered 1½–2-pint pie dish. Add the chopped onion and the milk. Cover with a buttered paper and bake in the centre of a moderate oven (355°F. – Gas Mark 4) for 15–20 minutes or until fish flakes.
3 Lift the fish fillets very carefully on to a warm serving platter. Strain the cooking liquor, make up to ⅓ pint if necessary and reserve. Set the fish aside to keep warm while preparing the sauce.
4 Melt the butter in a small saucepan over moderate heat and stir in the flour. Gradually add the milk, beating well all the time to get a really smooth sauce. Bring to the boil, and season with salt and pepper and allow to simmer gently for 2–3 minutes.
5 Add all but 1 tablespoon of the cheese and stir until melted and smooth. Pour the sauce over the fish and sprinkle with reserved cheese.
6 Pass under a hot grill until browned then serve at once with sauté potatoes and peas.

Lobster mayonnaise

you will need:

1 cooked lobster, cut in halves	½ small lettuce
salt	2–3 tablespoons mayonnaise
cayenne pepper	½ cucumber, sliced
lemon juice	1 hard-boiled egg

1 Crack open the lobster claws and remove the meat from the claws, halves and tail. Cut the flesh into small pieces or shred coarsely.
2 Discard the stomach found in the head section. Wash shells out thoroughly and dry.
3 Toss the meat with seasoning and a squeeze of lemon juice and set aside to marinate.
4 Wash the lettuce leaves, arrange on platter.
5 Blend the lobster meat with the mayonnaise and spoon back into the shells.
6 Arrange on the platter and garnish with cucumber slices and hard-boiled egg quarters.

Avocado dip

you will need:

2 ripe avocado pears	1 level teaspoon salt
8–9 oz. cream cheese	dash Worcestershire sauce
juice of ½ lemon	
1 teaspoon finely chopped onion	2 tablespoons cream or top of the milk

1 Halve the avocado pears, remove the stones and scoop out the flesh.

2 Mash well with a fork and add to the cream cheese along with remaining ingredients. Beat well until smooth and creamy.

3 Serve in a small basin surrounded with selection of biscuits suitable for dipping, small salty crackers and potato chips.

Party dip

you will need:

2 tablespoons French dressing	2 teaspoons finely chopped or grated onion
8 oz. cream cheese	
2 tablespoons tomato ketchup	1 teaspoon anchovy essence
	salt biscuits or potato crisps for serving

1 Gradually beat the French dressing into the cream cheese.

2 Add remaining ingredients and beat until smooth and creamy. Serve in a small bowl, surrounded with salty biscuits or potato chips.

Syllabub

you will need:

2 tablespoons white wine	1 tablespoon lemon juice
rind of $\frac{1}{2}$ lemon, finely grated	1 oz. castor sugar
	$\frac{1}{4}$ pint double cream

1 Combine together the wine, strained lemon juice, lemon rind and sugar in a basin. Leave to stand for 1 hour stirring occasionally.

2 Add the cream and whisk until the mixture is thick and light.

3 Spoon into two individual serving glasses and chill until ready to serve.

Variation

Banana syllabub – follow the recipe above, adding 2 well mashed bananas to the wine mixture before folding in the cream.

Zabaglione

you will need:

2 egg yolks	3 tablespoons Marsala wine or sweet sherry
2 oz. castor sugar	

1 Crack the egg yolks into a medium sized basin.

2 Add the sugar and Marsala wine or sherry to the yolks and place the basin over a saucepan, half filled with simmering water.

3 Whisk continuously until the mixture is thick and light.

4 Remove from the heat and pour into two individual serving goblets. Serve with sponge finger biscuits.

Caramel trifles

you will need:

2–3 sponge fingers	1 level tablespoon custard powder
1 tablespoon sweet sherry OR fruit juice	
	$\frac{1}{4}$ pint milk
for the custard:	$\frac{1}{8}$ pint double cream
2 rounded tablespoons castor sugar	
1 tablespoon water	**to decorate:**
	chopped walnuts

1 Break the sponge fingers into the base of two serving glasses. Sprinkle over the sherry or fruit juice and set aside while preparing the custard.

2 Measure half the sugar into a dry pan and place over moderate heat. Stir with a wooden spoon until sugar has melted and caramelised to a golden brown.

3 Draw the pan off the heat and add the water – take care because the liquid will steam furiously.

4 Allow to cool for 5 minutes. Meanwhile, in a small basin or cup, blend the custard powder with enough of the milk to make a thin paste.

5 Add remaining milk to the saucepan and stir over the heat until the caramel has dissolved and milk is almost boiling.

6 Pour over the blended custard powder, stirring well, then return to the saucepan and stir until the mixture is thickened and boiling. Add remaining sugar.

7 Allow the custard to cool, stirring occasionally to prevent a skin forming. Then spoon over the sponge fingers.

8 Whip the cream and spoon over the top. Sprinkle with chopped nuts and chill.

Sherry trifles

you will need:

2 trifle sponge cakes	$\frac{1}{2}$ pint milk
little red jam	1 level tablespoon castor sugar
1 tablespoon sherry	
1 large egg	$\frac{1}{4}$ pint double cream
1 level tablespoon cornflour	few toasted almonds

1 Halve the sponge cakes and spread with a little red jam. Cut into small pieces and arrange over the base of a small glass serving dish, sprinkle with sherry.

2 In a mixing basin, whisk the egg and cornflour together. Heat the milk to almost boiling and pour on to the egg mixture. Whisk thoroughly and strain back into the milk saucepan.

3 Stir over a low heat until thickened. Draw off the heat and stir in the castor sugar. Allow to cool a little, stirring occasionally.

4 Pour over the sponge cake and set aside until quite cold.

5 Whisk the cream until thick and spoon over the trifle; sprinkle with toasted almonds.

Baked peaches

you will need:

2 large fresh peaches

for the stuffing:
2 oz. ground almonds
2 oz. castor sugar

1 egg yolk
dash sweet sherry
4 small rounds sponge cake

1 Plunge the peaches into boiling water for 1 minute. Drain and peel away the skins; cut in halves and remove the stones.
2 In a basin combine together the ground almonds, sugar, egg yolk and enough sherry to make a moist consistency. Spoon into the hollow of each peach half.
3 Arrange the stuffed peaches in a well buttered baking dish.
4 Cover with a lid and place in the centre of a very moderate oven (355°F. – Gas Mark 4) and bake for 20 minutes.
5 Allow to become quite cold, then place each peach half on a round of sponge cake. Pour over any syrup from the baking dish and serve with single cream.

Bananas flambé

you will need:

1 oz. butter
2 oz. castor sugar
2–3 bananas

1 heaped tablespoon apricot jam
1 tablespoon rum

1 Heat the butter in a frying pan and stir in the sugar. Add the peeled bananas, that have been sliced lengthways.
2 Fry gently for 3–5 minutes until soft. Draw the pan off the heat and lift on to a hot serving dish.
3 Stir the apricot jam into the butter and sugar, and blend well.
4 Meanwhile warm the rum in a saucepan and put over very low heat.
5 Pour the apricot sauce over the bananas and pour over the warmed rum, set alight immediately and serve with cream.

Apricot brandy cream

you will need:

1 8-oz. tin apricot halves
¼ pint milk
1 oz. fine semolina
1 oz. castor sugar

1 egg, separated
1 tablespoon brandy or sherry

to decorate:
chopped walnuts

1 Spoon the drained tinned fruit into the bases of two individual glass serving dishes. Pour over a little of the fruit juice.
2 Heat the milk in a saucepan and sprinkle in the semolina. Bring to the boil, stirring occasionally, and cook for 2 minutes until thickened.
3 Draw the pan off the heat and stir in the sugar, egg yolk and brandy or sherry. Allow to cool 5–10 minutes.

4 Fold in the stiffly beaten egg white, spoon the mixture over the apricots and chill until ready to serve.
5 Sprinkle with chopped walnuts and serve with single cream.

Jam soufflé omelet

you will need:

3 eggs
2 level tablespoons castor sugar

1 oz. butter for frying
2 tablespoons red jam
icing sugar

1 Lightly whisk together the egg yolks and sugar in a basin set over a pan of hot, not boiling water until light.
2 Remove the basin from the heat and fold in the stiffly whisked egg whites.
3 Heat the butter in an 8-inch frying pan until bubbling hot. Add all the omelet mixture at once and spread evenly over the pan.
4 Cook over moderate heat for 1–2 minutes, long enough to allow the underside to brown lightly. Then place the pan in the centre of a pre-heated moderate oven (355°F. – Gas Mark 4) and cook for 10 minutes or until the omelet has risen and is firm to the touch.
5 Meanwhile warm the jam in a saucepan. Spread over the surface of the omelet as it comes from the oven. Fold the omelet in half, and put on a warm serving platter, sprinkle with icing sugar and serve immediately.

Variation

Rum soufflé omelet – follow the recipe above, adding 1 tablespoon rum to the egg yolks and sugar mixture in the first stage. While the omelet is cooking, heat a further 2–3 tablespoons rum very gently in a saucepan. Pour over the omelet after it has been turned out on to a serving dish, light immediately and serve at once.

Rum chocolate mousse

you will need:

2 oz. plain chocolate, broken in pieces

1 tablespoon rum
2 small eggs, separated

1 Place the chocolate in a small basin and set over a pan of hot water. Add the rum and stir until the chocolate has melted.
2 Remove the basin from the heat and stir in the egg yolks.
3 Whisk the egg whites until stiff and then gently fold into the chocolate mixture. Spoon into two individual serving glasses and chill until ready to serve.

Pears in red wine

you will need:

4 small medium-ripe pears
6 oz. castor sugar
¼ pint water
small piece stick cinnamon
¼ pint red wine

1 Peel the pears, but leave whole and with the stalks intact. Place close together in a small saucepan.
2 Add the sugar, water and cinnamon stick. Bring slowly to the boil then simmer gently covered with a lid for 15 minutes.
3 Remove the lid, add the red wine and cook gently for a further 15 minutes.
4 Lift the pears from the pan and place in a serving dish. Remove the cinnamon and continue to boil the syrup rapidly, until reduced to a light syrup.
5 Spoon over the pears and then put to chill for several hours before serving. Serve with cream.

Old English date pie

you will need:

3 oz. short crust pastry

for the filling:
1 teacup cut up dates
¼ pint single cream
2 small eggs
1 level teaspoon cinnamon
¼ level teaspoon nutmeg
pinch of cloves
pinch of salt
1 rounded tablespoon fresh white bread-crumbs
1 oz. desiccated coconut

1 Prepare the pastry – see page 4, and roll out to circle large enough to line a buttered 7–8 inch pie plate.
2 Sprinkle the sliced dates over the base of the pie.
3 Combine together all the remaining ingredients except the coconut, and beat well. Pour over the dates in the unbaked pastry case.
4 Place in the centre of a hot oven (400°F. – Gas Mark 6) and bake for 15 minutes. Then reduce the temperature to (355°F. – Gas Mark 3), sprinkle with the coconut and bake for a further 15 minutes or until the filling has set.
5 Cut in wedges and serve with single cream.

Index